Pardon me, Dearie— your values are showing

♥ ♥ ♥

RUTH MEAD

Tyndale House
Publishers, Inc.
Wheaton, Illinois

Dr. Dan Neuenschwander wrote all of chapter 7, "The Pretender," and certain other portions of the book. In addition, he supplied much information toward the development of my ideas. His advice and suggestions have been invaluable.

LIBRARY OF CONGRESS CATALOG CARD NUMBER 78-68905
ISBN 0-8423-4832-8, PAPER.
COPYRIGHT © 1979 BY RUTH MEAD.
ALL RIGHTS RESERVED.
TYNDALE HOUSE PUBLISHERS, INC.
WHEATON, ILLINOIS 60187.
FIRST PRINTING, AUGUST 1979.
PRINTED IN THE UNITED STATES OF AMERICA.

CONTENTS

INTRODUCTION

ONE
Jan
7

TWO
Looking for Love
20

THREE
"Response-Ability"
31

FOUR
The Achiever
46

FIVE
The Idealist
55

SIX
The Legalist
66

SEVEN
The Pretender
72

EIGHT
The Possessor
81

NINE
The Pleaser
89

TEN
Jan Returns
99

ELEVEN
Getting Ready for Love
108

TWELVE
Love: A Way of Seeing
114

LIST OF BOOKS
127

INTRODUCTION

Boy, does Jan have a problem. It's a problem that comes in the form of a million unanswered questions. She wonders, How can some people commit an entire life to the acquisition of material things which only have surface value? Why don't other people need to observe and listen to and understand their own experiences? How can people live for a career or for a family? Doesn't it seem, as Solomon says, that all is vanity?

Most people around Jan seem not to know that life has more meaning than this. They seem unable to recognize any needs except physical needs. And Jan knows that these people are considered nice guys by the society of which she's a part.

Jan isn't alone. Everywhere I look I see people struggling to fill this need for meaning in their lives. I see now that it is because the need for meaning and understanding is an actual *need*, necessary for the survival of one's own self.

It seems this urgent, terrible need would bind everyone together in the search for fulfillment. But many of us are discovering, as Jan did, that it's the sword that divides us. It isn't the need that divides us — what divides us is awareness or lack of awareness. Our sensitivity to the needs of that crying self (the early Church referred to it as the "spirit that craves for meaning and illumination") — that sensitivity determines what we do about our lives and how we shape our values.

On the one hand there is Jan who seems unable to shush the self that longs for a deeper meaning than that which she can find in marriage, in her children, or even in loving deeds. On the other hand are all the *nice* people—Johnny, her husband, and her parents and their friends—none of them suspecting there is more to life than what they can see, hear, or touch. But Jan is considered a malcontent; Johnny and friends are considered nice guys.

"Nice guys" stress behavior or appearances. Responsive people seek for love and a certain way of being. For the nice guys the surface stuff is "far out" and "wow." That's why they're such nice guys. They are predictable; they never change their viewpoint and we, society, *like* that. They don't challenge surface appearances.

Somehow Jan has been able to identify with love as the early believers defined it—not as actions, or helpfulness, or keeping rules, but as a way of being. She's able to identify with another doctrine basic to the early Church—the belief that in every man there is a person hidden in the unconscious realm (the heart) that sits alone in its prison and cries for meaning. St. Thomas refers to the human spirit as "the principle of understanding and freedom." Merton defines the human spirit as "the intelligence as a principle either of speculation or of practical understanding." Their belief was that the human spirit is dead when it is unresponsive—unresponsive to the things of God—but that this human spirit could be awakened to the spiritual realm. Love was a person who came to live with the human spirit, uniting himself with man's spirit ("He who cleaves to the Lord is one spirit with him, penetrating and enlightening his understanding").

This love is reflected in the believer as the Spirit of God penetrates and enlightens the human spirit in the ways of freedom: freedom from legalism, self-defense, hypocrisy, closedness, idealism, and feverish activity.

This book attempts to understand Jan's problem and her search for meaning. It tries to identify "ego-traps"—ways in which people avoid responding in love. Finally, it examines how responsive love is a whole new way of seeing.

ONE
JAN

My friend, Jan, moved away from Munich a while back. One morning shortly before she left she buzzed over for coffee.

Even before she had taken her coat off, she was wailing, "I can't stand this zilch marriage anymore. If I have to live like this much longer I'll go out and do something neurotic. Or join a convent."

I look at her frozen, stormy face. "Well," I say, "if you join a convent, then I won't have to listen to you gripe about your fat knees anymore. That's *one* good thing. Really, Jan, what's the matter with you and Johnny?"

Jan tosses her green stocking cap on the couch and gives her fiery red hair a frenzied toss. "Listen," she says. "I'm sorry, kid, but love is what it's about. It's the only thing that matters. Life doesn't begin until you find it and it dies when you lose it. And, right now, I don't have it. That's all I know."

Jan settles into the rust-orange easy chair, pulls her legs up, and curls into a ball. "Gee," she says, "I feel like Typhoid Mary. I feel like some horrid misfit that can't find meaning in anything everyone else finds meaningful."

Jan slows down and takes a deep breath. "Well," she says finally, with a sort of despairing smile on her face, "what should I expect from a society where this year's husband is next year's Christmas card from Peoria?"

"Quit being funny," I warn. "It's anti-feminine."

Jan, as usual, is unrepentant for the fact that she is herself. "I hear that only ugly girls or handicapped girls develop a sense of humor," she once said. "That lets me in on both counts."

Jan bites her lower lip, which she does when she isn't *quite* sure how to say something. "I mean if we were simply dating, it would be different. If there was nothing meaningful going on between us, I could simply bug off. Pronto. Or go home to Mummy. But driving off in my little red station wagon, my hair flying in the wind, with three kids? I mean *forget* it!

"Besides, I really wonder about love. I get so tired of all this. People fall on their stupid faces over someone, and then two months later you find those same two people who once were quivering with lust or desire for each other, now not only definitely *not* quivering, but obviously not able to stand the sight of each other."

"Sometimes," I say. "Sometimes not. Sometimes it simply turns into routine and ho-hum and wondering if you're unreasonable to expect a little more — mmmmmm, *response* might be the word. So you argue with yourself a lot, tell yourself that no, it's not demanding too much to want response, to want something to respond *to*. At least it's not too much to expect from your husband. After all, you tell yourself, you're not asking for the world. You're not talking miracles. You don't expect Senator Klutz to answer your letter of inquiry personally or Robert Mitchum to comfort you on your mother's death."

Jan is laughing. That's one thing I like about Jan. She's like a boy I went to school with in third grade. Anything I'd say, he'd laugh. I'd say "boo" — he'd laugh. I'd say "hi" — he'd laugh. He not only laughed — he'd hold his sides laughing. He'd go round up the other kids on the playground, run back and beg, "Do it again. Go ahead. Say 'boo.' It makes me laugh."

Anyway, you'd like Jan. You would. She's so human. She's normally not the super-critical type she's already coming off sounding here — the type that whines, whines, whines because she sees herself as Victim, the person who gets the neck of the chicken and the rumble seat ride. Or the type who plays Psychiatrist, making harsh judgments like "the reason Mrs. Vanwarmer eats so much is because she's greedy." Or "the reason Ernie Smernie brags on himself is because he feels inferior." Or "the reason Raymond Ramrod criticizes others is because he's trying to bring people down to his level."

And she doesn't confuse smothering with love. She might tell her ten-year-old it's cold outdoors, but she probably wouldn't tell him to wear a mackinaw and stocking cap, knowing he'd have enough sense to figure it out for himself and that, anyway, he wouldn't die if he got cold. I mean, she allows room for people to grow.

But she can also criticize. Jan has the ability to reject the ideas a person holds without rejecting the person who holds those ideas. You know the warning Solomon gave? He who rebukes a scorner better get ready for abuse, and he who reproves a wicked man better be within a walking distance of a hospital; but if you rebuke a wise man, he will love you all the more. Well, Solomon would have put Jan in the Wise category. She hates Pretend Honesty. I found the hard way that if you just go on smiling when you totally disagree with the way Jan sees something, she's positively livid.

When I remarked on that quality in her, thinking it was pretty neat, she said, "Look, kid. If a person values his physical life, would he get mad at the doctor if the doctor told him he had cancer? Would he yell, 'Look, you aren't perfect either, Doc — look at that big goiter hanging off your neck'?"

And here's another thing about Jan I haven't found in too

many friends. Have you noticed that if you mention something you observe about a person's pattern of thinking—maybe even the way he flings his hands around when he talks—that person will actually try to change the thing you observe? As if *your* noticing or observing demands *their* doing something about what is observed. Not Jan. When you see something new in her, she acts like she's found a hundred-dollar bill. It's as if she knows that observing and seeing and noticing are ways of caring.

You can tell I've gotten off the subject. As far as Jan and Johnny are concerned, I can remember when Jan and Johnny were lovers of the year. Everything about Johnny was wonderful. Johnny's wonderful build. Johnny's wonderful parents. Johnny's wonderful blue jeans.

"It's the same old idiot story," Jan fumes. "I have it nice. Security and a nice house and nice kids. And respectability. And yet I feel empty. I keep looking for something gone wrong. 'You're really a lucky dog,' I keep telling myself, 'you're really lucky. Shame on you for being so unappreciative.'

"So I straighten up a while. But then it's like some never-ending merry-go-round. It starts all over again. Then I try to remember the hospital with all the crippled children and remember what beautiful-neat kids we have. Or I smile a lot. Or do nice things for people.

"But when I'm all through and come back home to myself, there I am, this other self deep inside, still waiting and crying."

Jan looks ashamed.

"Go ahead," I say. "You'd better deal with your feelings. They're probably trying to tell you about real needs."

If there's one thing that ties everything together about Jan, it would be a relentless internal mechanism that automatically mulls things over, breaks them down, until that idea or event is absorbed and made part of her personality. It's as if this mechanism *has* to put things together into some meaningful whole or else Jan can't bear to live.

"I'm clawing like a desperate animal to scratch out some meaning in life and suddenly I look up and won't believe my eyes. There's Johnny, concerned only with appearances, smoothing things over, keeping busy, making as much money as possible, concerned with nice words, surface relationships. While I grow away from material possessions—I guess I don't really trust them—I look up and he's busy learning new manipulations to get what he wants or keep what he has. . . .

"*I* must be the crazy one," Jan wails. "No one else seems to have my needs. I've watched Johnny, observed him, asked him. No, he doesn't need to understand what's behind anything, doesn't understand why I need anything except a nice house and a nice family. . . .

"And I try to tell him it isn't a career I want, because it isn't. I've had that and I don't want it, at least right now. I *like* being home with the kids. It's something a lot deeper. . . .

"And it didn't used to bother me that we couldn't go any deeper than safe talk. Now I think it's going to kill me. Like last evening I sort of went crazy. There we were—being our nice selves and suddenly I wanted to talk about a particular experience I was having and what it might be trying to show me. He said that understanding is stupid, a bunch of suppositions—all that matters is action. Whenever I start talking these days he pulls down this curtain between us, which means he isn't going to respond or think about it or have any feedback to give me on the subject. In his nice, quiet way he is in control and we will *not* discuss this situation or any situation. Period. Not unless I bring something up—at which time I'll talk about it until I weary of the sound of my own voice, like waves beating against a stone wall.

"And suddenly last night I thought I couldn't stand a minute more of that surface stuff. I really thought it was going to kill me."

We have wandered into the kitchen. But Jan now rescues her cap from the living room couch, and returns with it over her face. She stumbles around the room, goofing off as usual. She sits down on the step-up to the kitchen, hangs her head down, her hair falling over her face, as if she wants to hide from her problems.

"Ever read any books on marriage?" I offer. Weakly. Very weakly.

"Face it, kid, I mean face it." Jan runs her fingers through her hair and lets it fall over her face. Her green eyes appear and disappear as she pulls her hair back, then lets it fall again. "A good marriage today means being nice and accepting, and it means conniving to get more material things from your husband. Or it's some open deal in which you go on being single, both of you, but sharing the same house and bed, in which case each other's feelings and thoughts and values don't matter so much.

"Marriage books tell you how to make lists and get your housework done; but all any of us need is some *reason* to get our housework done. I don't think any of us can just go on indefinitely, having babies so they, in turn, can have babies so they, in turn, can have babies—see what I mean?

"Those authorities don't think there's a problem in marriage except who's going to be boss. I guess they've interpreted that thing about the man being the head of the family to mean the *boss* of the family, if you can imagine that. I tell 'em, 'Okay, fine. That's already established at our house. I hate being boss. What I want is a relationship. *Now* what do I do?' and then they come unglued. They haven't memorized an answer to that, you know."

Jan is normally the funny-girl type, but when she's having an attack of intensity like this, looking for roots and causes, she reminds me of Little Bo Peep. Not looking for sheep, of course. Just looking. Trying to make sense out of things. And if it's true that the truth will make you free, but first it will make you miserable, then it's clear to me that Jan is in the Miserable stage of her search.

Listening to Jan, I was sitting there thinking of the paradox of it all. What I'd read of Abraham Maslow's postulate—"The need to understand is a real need requiring real fulfillment"— didn't jibe with all those people I know who don't care about understanding life—*comprehension*. Yet every so often someone, like Jan, proves Maslow's postulate true; and their restlessness is with the lack of response in people. They can't tolerate the drugged apathy of modern life.

"However," Jan is ready to go on now, "I'll tell you something. I'd really like to pin this problem I'm having on marriage, but it occurred to me just recently that this problem is the same old ugly problem I've always had—even before marriage—only now in an unrecognizable form."

I don't understand what she means.

"Well, see here," she says, "I've always been pretty sure there's something wrong with me. I can't give a darn about what other people give *lots* of darns about. Even back in school I'd try to care about football games or parties or fun stuff—and I'd see everyone else obviously caring and I'd think, 'They've got to be kidding—they *can't* care. They've got to be *acting* like they care.'"

Jan wanders to the living room again, wondering aloud if her kids had made the school bus. "What I mean is that here I am again—same problem. No problems about money. No problems about anything, really. Only that same old problem of not caring about what other people care about. Johnny and I don't agree at all about what matters. Or what's really important. Not at all," she sniffs.

"Oh," I say. It was all I could muster.

"And like I said," Jan continues, "I've always had this problem. Not only with Johnny, but with lots of people. All of them nice, wonderful, very nice, respectable, nice people. And up to now I've gone along pretty much believing them and blaming myself. I've been expecting them to prove that the things they're good at (remembering names, packing school lunches, organizing, making wrinkle-free beds) are important, and things they're *not* good at (understanding, caring, openness, realness) are not important."

Jan is like me in this way. She doesn't know what she's going to say before she says it. She never seems to know what she thinks until she thinks out loud or on paper. "I don't know why I'm remembering this," she says, "but we got a box of silver for our wedding present. It had come from the East and the knife rack was slightly cracked. When I showed the silver to him, he noticed the crack right away and said we couldn't accept it. And I said, 'But look at this stuff. Isn't it lovely?' And he said, 'We can't accept broken merchandise.' And I kept saying don't be silly and how could a broken rack be half as bad as ingratitude and who cares about a silly old box—and all he said was, 'I do. I care about the box. My wife is only going to have the best.' And I said, 'Define best.' Well, he's been doing that ever since.

"He thinks missing church is wrong. I think defensiveness is wrong. He thinks saying 'darn' is wrong. I think constant evasiveness is wrong. To him behavior and appearances are the most important things. To me talking about ideas and premises and concepts—all this root stuff—is terribly important. He thinks it's wrong. Really wrong. Because it's a waste of time. To Johnny hypocrisy and lying don't matter as much as not putting a tricycle away. Or as much as incorrect grammar. . . .

"Randy talked to Johnny last night. Randy said, 'I didn't

understand nothing about . . . .' Immediately Johnny corrected him in a freezing tone. 'I didn't understand anything, a-n-y-t-h-i-n-g. . .' Johnny said. Randy said, 'Okay.' But now he's nervous and fidgety. He knows that *what* he has to say is of no importance. Only his *way* of saying things is important. Johnny succeeded in correcting his grammar, but made him self-conscious in the process.

"If I want openness, Johnny thinks I mean 'saying words,' so he begins to torture me with a long description of a power plant or something. And if I complain, he says, 'See, you wanted me to talk and now look what happens. I can't please you.'

"It's like we're from different planets."

Jan's breath catches like a child's after a temper tantrum or a good, hard cry. Suddenly she jumps to her feet. "Hey," she says, "not that your coffee isn't good—but let's go to the Wienerwald."

So we head to the Wienerwald together. This is as close as our friendship comes to a ritual. Maybe this cold air makes us think. Or maybe it's the strong, black, German coffee that warms our conversation.

It's a drizzly morning and the deep dark pines are drenched, but we manage a flow of chatter as we walk, huddled in trench coats. I notice for the first time how seldom we talk about self-discovery—but how often we talk about *what* the self discovers and sees and understands.

Today the Wienerwald seems even warmer and homier than usual. The bronze antique lanterns are lit and they flicker over the red checkered tablecloths that cover the tables. There is no need to place an order. The Norwegian *ober* already hustles around, filling two small steel pots of coffee and nodding his greetings. Jan seems not to notice the surroundings. . . .

"I guess I feel like I don't know what's important anymore.

Like I've lost my way and don't know where to find it. I've become so disenchanted with my parents and their friends — these are people I thought I could look up to for guidance. They're at least twenty-five years older than I am. But the things that seem important to them are so trivial. They're so binky. So *nothing*."

Jan is right. I had met one of Jan's parents' "set" in the grocery line once. You know — the type of woman you have to explain jokes to. Someone who brushes dandruff off people's shoulders while she talks to them. Her greatest joy was that her daughter-in-law finally (after months of nagging) called her "Mother."

"Isn't 'Mother' a beautiful word?" she gurgled to me, her eyes glowing. "You have a mother's heart, so you know what it means to me."

"Goodness, I don't know," I hedged. "Someday, if and when I have a daughter-in-law, and if we *like* each other, I guess I wouldn't really care if she called me Maude. Or Clarabelle. Or anything."

She suddenly appears crestfallen, and I want to kick myself. "Oh," she moaned, "how very disrespectful that would be."

"And just look," Jan is saying, "these are grown women. They never examine the selfishness motivating their lives. They praise each other for stupid, unimportant things. They never bother to look up from their frantic work of impressing others to notice that their supposed audience isn't paying any attention to them or noticing the name Givency scribbled on their scarves. I couldn't care a hoot if their skin is toned by Eva of Roma. After I'm around them a while I'd do anything to see someone a little sloppy. Or quirky. Or crabby. At least *alive*."

I asked Jan about her dad, knowing how fond she is of her dad. I asked her if he was any different.

"My *dad?*" Jan seems close to tears and I wish I hadn't asked the question. "Gee, my dad is neat, but I wouldn't go to him for guidance. Dad doesn't notice much of anything as long as I keep a sweet smile on my face. And he likes me to wear a dress rather than blue jeans. A dress," Jan laughs through near-tears. "To Dad, my wearing a dress is very important. It symbolizes femininity. He's super impressed with surfaces."

"It's as if they had no faith—" I begin.

"Faith?" Jan asks, suddenly cold. "What does faith have to do with anything?"

"Well, you know that self you said was still crying when you come back home to it? Well, faith is the attitude of that self— faith searches for causes and meaning and enlightenment; it searches out the invisible behind the visible."

"Listen," Jan says, "any question I've ever asked religious people was silenced by 'have faith.' I *hate* faith."

"Gee, Jan," I wince, "that makes me feel awful. I mean faith asks questions for *exactly* the reason that it knows there are answers. The man without faith won't ask questions because he doesn't believe there are answers. Like he doesn't want to embarrass poor God with questions God can't answer. . . .

"Faith doesn't mean to open yourself to the facts that fit in with your preconceived ideas. It means giving up your ego, your preconceived ideas, so you are free to open yourself to what is actually there.

"A woman could love her husband, a man his wife—but that love won't necessarily be rewarded with love-in-return, as silly, naive women are teaching today, any more than God's love for man was rewarded with love-in-return. All the love in the world won't make a dent without faith. Faith is the receiver of love."

Jan is quiet for a while, knotting and unknotting the heavy

rusty-red linen napkin. "I always thought faith meant hanging on to some premise you've been taught even if it goes against all logic. . . .

"You said once," Jan says slowly, measuring words, "that the human spirit is the seer in me. If that's true, then people without faith, who aren't open to what's behind behavior, who never care to see or understand the principles that guide life — well, in a way you could call them 'emotional virgins.'"

Jan is absently but ponderously stirring the dregs in the bottom of her coffee cup. "I'll tell you what this surface stuff feels like to me," she says. "It feels cold and dead and depriving and all black and barbed-wiry and scary to me."

"Have any idea what you're looking for?" I finally ask, seeing the enormity of the problem.

"Let me tell you," Jan says. "I had a really super teacher once. She was one of those old maid, flat-chested types that wore the same two jersey dresses all year, one a green polka-dot and one a blue polka-dot, made exactly alike. She said that becoming a loving person was the greatest thing anyone could ever want from life. And that seemed so right and simple at the time and I knew that's what I wanted.

"And then I saw everyone *using* love to simply get a happy marriage or a new fur coat or some other thing they wanted. They'd be submissive to get less argument, more goodies. They'd want insight only so they could be more interesting to other people. Let me tell you something, kid — something sort of snapped in me. All of a sudden I wanted to run somewhere and throw up. Now this whole loving thing makes me want to scream."

"Aw, Jan, c'mon," I plead, "there's a pseudo-*everything*. And besides, truth won't reveal itself to the person who wants to manipulate it, but only to the one who loves it for itself. To the early believers, love was a new heart, a whole way of being. It had to do with motive. Love is motive. Love is the only motive with no ulterior motive. So the very *opposite* of real love is actually all those ulterior motives you're talking about."

But what I say isn't much help.

"Well, see here," Jan says, "it all makes me so sick I want to do something desperate. Now I'm not sure about anything."

TWO
LOOKING FOR LOVE

The next time I saw Jan, she was in the American bookstore furiously rifling through the pages of a magazine. She yelled across the store, beckoned me to come to the magazine rack, and we talked as she sheepishly resumed her obvious search.

Jan can't keep a secret no matter how hard she tries, and she finally burst into embarrassed laughter. "Gee, this really makes me feel stupid," she groans, "but I'm looking for a picture of Goldie Hawn."

I just look at her. "Good grief. What *for?*" I say. "Gonna put it on your piano?"

Jan looks ridiculous. "Look," she says, "don't laugh. Promise not to laugh?"

I assume a poker face. Solemnly I raise my right hand, place my left hand reverently on a book.

"Okay, you promised. I'll kill you if you laugh. Johnny wants me to look like Goldie Hawn."

I shriek with laughter. "Are you kidding? *You?* Look like Goldie Hawn? You're kidding. You have red hair. Curves. I mean you couldn't. You could *never* look like Goldie Hawn. Besides, you'd need a lobotomy."

Jan isn't laughing. She is drumming her fingers on the book

rack. "Goldie Hawn," she repeats, wiping a piece of imaginary dust off the jacket of a dog-eared copy of *Vogue*. "Goldie Hawn," she repeats flatly. Very flatly. "Think about it a while, kid. Goldie Hawn. Maybe Johnny knows he can't love me as I am. Maybe he can't love me because I exist. Because I'm real. Maybe he hates reality and loves only what his own imagination creates."

"Well," I say, "why don't you run up to Johnny and yell so loudly he has to cover his ears, 'Look, Johnny, it's me. Jan. Me! See, it's me. Look at me. This hunk of flesh standing before you is me. Jan. Is there any way you could love me?'"

"Oh, he'd say 'sure.' He would. He'd say 'sure.' Only thing, he wouldn't know what I was talking about. Remember those stories about a person going into a coma, and this person wouldn't ever recognize the one standing by his bed who loved him so much? Well, maybe it's that way a lot. Maybe a lot of us don't know. Don't recognize who anyone really is."

"There's a song like that," I think aloud. "An old spiritual. 'Sweet little Jesus boy. Lay in a manger. And we didn't know who he wuz.'"

Jan switches the subject and wonders aloud if there's anything in the world that can be an end in itself without it running from you. "It seems the minute I try to make marriage or possessions or humanity or anything else the Most Important Thing—I right away begin feeling insecure and afraid because I know this stuff is going to pass away and I'm going to be left holding the gunnysack.

"Even happiness. Happiness is important. Wow, is it important. But when I make it the end I run toward, then not only do I miss out on happiness, but everything else as well."

I'd noticed the same thing. It's one of those principles you just stand back and observe for a long time without really understanding why it should work that way. Like you can see that the person who constantly sends out conscious and unconscious messages of "approve of me, notice me, pay attention to me" is eventually ignored, but you don't understand why.

What I had been noticing was that what you love and respond to is so important that it determines everything in life. What I love (my values) determines why I love (my motive) and who I love. "Guard your affections—for out of your affections flow the issues of life," is the way an early Bible writer put it. I mentioned this to Jan.

Jan stands there for a moment, thinking. "Take Marge," she says. "When she got on the Happy Marriage kick, I thought it was a passing sickness like all her other sicknesses. But it's affected everything about her now—even her relationships.

"She's so quick with superficial answers to other people's marriage problems, so blaming, so closed on the subject of marriage that her friends and former friends run when they see her coming. She'd be more popular with incurable psoriasis or halitosis.

"She suddenly got even *more* defensive of Rex, when no one in his right mind would think of attacking Rex or even breathing unevenly in his presence. She's arrogant about what she labels her 'Happy Marriage,' even to the point of having a Secret Key to her marriage. ('The reason I have such a happy marriage is because I'm so appreciative and accepting.') It's colored *everything*."

Jan picks up a book, flips through it, clears her throat a few times, wanting desperately to appear nonchalant. "Hey, does religion have anything to say about marriage principles?" she finally blurts, contemplating her future, I imagine.

I'm standing there with my mouth hanging open—thinking.

"Will you please close your mouth?" Jan laughs. She's warned me about this before—that if I don't stop doing that when I'm deep in thought, she will refuse to be seen with me in public.

"You could take the principle 'Materialism in one of its thousand forms is the root of all evil' and apply it to marriage. If I'm a materialistic woman, I'm definitely going to be unable to love my husband and children. I don't hate my husband or kids by really hating them, but by preferring what they can do for me. But, well, the truth is that there are no marriage principles. A principle is a universal law that applies to life, and since marriage is a specific thing, there's no such thing as a marriage principle."

"Well, hey," Jan clears her throat again. "You don't suppose there's some principle that would apply to my problem, is there?"

I had to think a while. I had been more and more awakened to the fact that when I'm working on a relationship, what I'm really working on is saving my own neck. My own security. And that, odd as it seemed, the more I tried to save my security here on earth, the more I lost the inner security that isn't dependent on anything in my environment.

"The principle that requires the most daring is, 'Seek first the kingdom of heaven and everything else will be thrown in as a bonus without making it important.' Which also implies that even if you did somehow manage a really super marriage by spending every minute from breakfast to midnight working on a happy relationship, someday that self deep inside you would be crying again. You'd be left holding the gunnysack. You'd still be stuck with this self you'd been ignoring all this time.

"Actually if you want to know the truth, I think it was pretty kind of one old saint to warn against our preferring the world, setting our sights on something that doesn't last (even if it's marriage). He wanted to save us from the living hell of aloneness, where we discover that 'the world passes away'—and so does marriage. What I'll be stuck with forever is myself."

Jan misunderstood at first. Said she didn't believe in ignoring problems. And I said I don't either, but what I am 100 percent for is making the reckless blind leap, not once, but perpetually, from preoccupation with my own outer problems to preoccupation with the inner process. I rest on the promise that if I occupy myself with this inner journey, refusing to idolize marriage, take its temperature daily, baby it, coddle it—well, that the outer problems will take care of themselves.

I told her that if she really wanted to find out what faith is, she could find out soon enough by hurling herself on a principle like this. And she'd also find out that a principle is not an idea, but so real you can walk on it, so substantial you can put your whole weight on it and let yourself go.

I guess that appealed to Jan, that idea of recklessness because she hates the spit-curl, every-hair-in-place, tight-corset way of thinking, and personally I think she liked the idea of love being a journey. First, because she's been wanting to pack her big brown suitcase for a long time. And second, because she's attracted to growth and process and perception and insight. She is repulsed by stagnation and rigidity and blindness and instant-anything, which I guess leads us right back to spit-curls and tight corsets.

"What did you mean by 'the kingdom of heaven'?" Jan asks. I had forgotten already that I'd used the phrase.

"Love," I say simply.

"You're making it simple again," Jan raises a warning eyebrow. It's her drop-dead look.

"Simple?" I croak, remembering how many answers to the kingdom of heaven I'd actually had to live through before I could see what awful impostors they were. I recalled how things began to come together when my first priority became the search for meaning or wisdom.

Suddenly I feel self-conscious. Two guys in the aisle have stopped reading. One is holding an Erica Jong book mid-air, and is staring at his heavy argyle socks tucked into German sandals. The other hasn't turned a page since about page three. It's funny how people stop and listen when they hear the word "love" or "God." I've noticed it quite often.

"Listen, Jan, if you understood what the old masters of the Way meant by love and what they meant by 'being a loving person,' you'd know how *un*-simple—"

"Listen, kid, if it's anything like what Ronda's pastor means by love—forget *it*. He smiles all the time like a pumpkin. So I ask him why he's smiling all the time and he says he's glad I asked. Says he smiles to show how much Jesus loves everyone. Well, *darn*, it had all been lost on me. I was going to prescribe Pepto-Bismol. He always looked to me like a baby with gas."

(I'm sorry if you think I'm sacrilegious, but that's me—over there groaning with laughter, leaning on a book rack for support.) I recover my composure before Jan finishes. "See," she says, "it's real easy for these Christians. All they have to do is say yes to Jesus, memorize John 3:16, and go on being as selfish and materialistic and closed and as dumb, dumb, dumb as they want because they now have Salvation. Salvation has nothing to do with motives or responses or understanding. It's a written guarantee. An insurance policy. All paid up."

Slowly the light dawns. "So *that's* it. That's it with you, isn't it?" I say. "Janice is turned off by shallowness. What do you know? That's why you prefer being the good agnostic. Look, Jan, really, listen to me. If one of our modern, materialistic professors of Christianity would have told old St. Bernard how much he loved Jesus, the old man would have peered out at him through his thick glasses, wrinkled his nose, and said, 'Tell me *what* you love, brother, and I'll tell you if you love God!' He said there were three kinds of religious men—subjective people who love God because God is good to them and loads them down with goodies. This guy loves his own security and comfort. Then there are people who love God because God is powerful. This is the person who's really in love with power, but thinks he loves God. Then there's the third man who loves God because he loves God. No ulterior motive. He loves God because God is *good*. This unselfish love with no ulterior motive is what 'pure in heart' is all about."

Jan blinks. "It *is?*" she says. "I always figured pure-in-heart had something to do with old maids in high-necked dresses or cameos bobbing up and down on black, virginal habits."

Jan suddenly becomes serious. She's just *standing* there. Staring at me.

"What's the matter?"

"Where have you been getting all this stuff?" she asks.

"I didn't want to tell you," I whisper hoarsely, looking over the shelves furtively, hoping to arouse Jan's hatred of religion-as-a-form-of-irrationality, "but I hear voices from the woodwork."

She laughs. "It's those old, green, yukky, mildewy, icky books from London you've been going through. They make me wretch just to look at them."

"*Digging* through," I correct. "You're right. I've been trying to find what the early Church meant by love. Dan's been digging through the ones he can find in the States on the subject. I've been haunting the old English shops and giving those books a workover. It's like finding treasure hidden from the world for nearly two thousand years. Tell you one thing — any similarity between what *they* meant by love and what *we* mean by it is purely accidental. See you around," I say, heading for the cash register.

"Gee, you're abrupt," Jan scolds. "I never get over how abrupt you are. Wait outside just a minute. Be right there. Goldie Hawn be hanged."

I think I've spent most of my life looking for a place to sit down. I wander to the far end of the top step to sit down in the bright winter sunlight; I watch the Americans away from home drifting in and out of the store. (There's something appalling about the way Americans dress away from home, as if they think no one will look at them until they get back to the States.)

Jan stumbles out the door, shielding her eyes from the bright sunlight with one hand, and realizes she has lost her hat. She collides head-on with an enormous lady with perfectly stacked hair and trembling chins.

After she finds the slightly-trampled hat, she crumbles beside me on the step, sitting on her gloved hands. Then she leans forward, her shoulders hunched, rocks back and forth on her hands a few times getting ready to say something.

"If I really believed I could grow in any situation, it would determine a lot of other things for me," she states.

Now, I think in images rather than words and when I think of St. Paul advising early believers to "stay put" in their situations, whether it be marriage or slavery, I remember the trees my father once had sent home with me to transplant in my own yard. I remember how much energy had been expended in simply putting roots down and surviving changes in the environment. Likewise, I wonder if a person doesn't have to forget about the outer life at least for a while until the inner life is well-rooted. Anyway, I say to Jan that according to the early believers it wasn't wrong to free yourself from impossible situations. It was, however, clear that freeing yourself (even from slavery) can't be your main aim. I make the point that love isn't dependent on anything in the external world but is a quality of life, of *response* from within, flowing outward. That's why people can't understand it—the source of response isn't external, it's internal.

So, years ago people looked at the responsive believer and said, "Hey, how *come*? He was raised in the same town I was.

He doesn't have enough turnips for his next meal either. If I had to live with his wife I'd kill myself. This doesn't make sense—doesn't make any sense at all. What makes him tick?"

Anyone with the courage to simply open his eyes had to admit that these people weren't formed by their environments, or conformed to anyone they lived with, but transformed from somewhere inside themselves. People even suspected that Someone inside these people taught them because here were people with no discernible teachers who grew by leaps and bounds in intelligence. And this wasn't the head kind of intelligence that memorizes, makes rules, and lives by shoulds, coulds, and might be's. But it was the heart kind of comprehension, called perception and understanding. Love then was known to be the highest form of intelligence.

"The neat thing about the kingdom of heaven being inside me rather than coming from my environment is that no one in the world can separate me from love," I finish. "Love was, they believed, a person who came to eat and drink, and talk to a human spirit that was poor and needy. Like Mary and Jesus—Mary would show Jesus an image of the way she was seeing something and he'd spend hours at a time if she wanted, helping to clarify and broaden and deepen her understanding—get it more in line with reality."

"He did that?" Jan asks, incredulous. "He took the time to do that?"

"Sure—there was no seeking for emotion for emotion's sake. Insight into the nature and work and ways of God was where their joy came from—joy so tangible you could almost laugh and play and run in it."

"I've known since I was a little kid that anything exciting or wonderful that was ever going to come to me had to happen inside," Jan says.

"Another neat thing about the inside business is that it removes all fear of people and circumstances," I think aloud. "No person can prevent me from being reborn or destroy my unique way of seeing things. Or prevent my growth away from preoccupation with the outside of things to caring about things of substance and worth. No person can touch the fact that truth will continue to reveal itself to me if I want it to."

"Something inside me knows all of that is true," Jan murmurs, "and maybe if I could talk to that old maid teacher again—maybe she meant something like, 'The only way to be a loving person is simply to be the right kind of person so I can just be *myself* with no striving, pretenses, hypocrisy, or defenses.' But I still wouldn't know how to be that kind of person."

That's one of Jan's ways of asking a question, but nothing comes to me right away. I sit and watch my breath in the cold air. "Well, let's see. Maybe you could compare it to being a Norwegian. Acting like a Norwegian wouldn't make you a Norwegian. Talking like a Norwegian, learning the language, putting on a heavy overcoat or earmuffs, or learning to ski isn't going to make you more and more Norwegian. Even drinking twelve cups of strong coffee a day won't cut it. . . ."

"Guess you'd have to be born—" Jan begins. Then she catches her own implication, so she finishes swiftly, "—to Norwegians."

Now I don't know if Jan ever comes to conclusions. Conclusions, I think, come to her. And suddenly a conclusion seems to have broken through into her consciousness about something-or-other. She jumps to her feet and we begin walking down the path toward her bike.

"Ever heard of Simone Weil?" I question.

"Simone who?"

"Never mind. She was a searcher for truth. Like you, you know. She wrote lots of beautiful things. She said that Christ likes us to prefer the truth in life because before being Christ, he was truth. That if one turns aside from Christ to go toward truth, one will not go far before falling into his arms."

"That's sort of pretty," Jan says. "Things are going to be okay somehow, kid," she says with something like certainty. She takes her green stocking cap from her pocket, jams it on her head, tucks her hair under it and pedals off, waving as she rides away.

As I watch her clogs slowly peddle down the cobblestone street, her dead-earnest search for meaning seems as prophetic of joy as a rosebud is prophetic of the rose to come. And the words, "He who seeks will surely find," are the basis for my certainty.

THREE
"RESPONSE-ABILITY"

EGO-TRAPS

Did I tell you that Jan moved back to the States? Texas, if you want to know. And I didn't see her again until recently, which I'll tell you about later.

Jan had found she couldn't live without love. She had begun to question the meaning of love. And after she left, everywhere I'd look I'd see Jan's problem in different forms. Abraham Maslow wrote: "If this essential core of the person is denied or suppressed, he gets sick—sometimes in obvious ways, sometimes in subtle ways, sometimes immediately, sometimes later." He lists many of the problems that are "violent reactions against the frustration of our intrinsic needs, emotions, and capacities. . . ."

On the other hand, I saw Johnnys everywhere—seemingly satisfied people. These surface people at one time were just unwilling to respond to life-in-general (to observe, listen, look for meaning, and come to authentic conclusions); now they were unable to respond at all. A total tune-out. No inner dialogue. No questioning. No looking. No interpretation. These were people whose responses were dried up at the roots.

Most of all, these people had lost touch with what the early believers knew to be man's only *real* responsibility—

"response-ability." The ability to respond. Some modern thinkers agree: Dr. Perls writes, "Responsibility is the ability to respond. This is I believe the most basic characteristic of the mature person."

Well, when you tell someone like Jan that Christianity goes so far beyond shallowness and niceness and surfaces, and that it shoots right into the realm of response, you'd better have done your homework and not be merely mouthing words, because Jan was born with a baloney detector that won't quit. So I told her how far we've come from the central theme of Christianity.

The early believers didn't confuse sin with health hazards like smoking seaweed or getting drunk on fermented pickle juice. The only real sin—because it was the root of every sin—was the refusal to respond. It was obedience—a seeking, meditating, responding obedience—that God demanded, not bootlicking obedience. Not blind obedience.

And cloaking this passivity and irresponsibility in church activities would have been comparable to the way a frigid, tight-lipped woman, who is unable to respond to her husband, subconsciously tries to make up for her coldness by scrubbing his Big Macs every day by hand and ironing them from drippy wet to dry.

The early Christians got their terrific energy from facing the truth, meditating on the message, contemplating the meaning rather than misusing their energy like the one-talent servant did—in suppression of truth. Thomas Merton wrote: "In fallen man action is the desperate anodyne for a soul that knows instinctively it was made for contemplation."

Well, what it all seems to add up to is that action isn't the only substitute we've thought up for response. There are thousands of forms of evasions and substitutes, the forms of *stuckness* being as many and varied as the people looking for them. There's legalism and idealism and pretending.

There's self-protection—like the little boy next door who describes his uncle: "He's a real jerky guy that plays Scrabble and stuff like that all the time and teaches you how to be careful about what you say so no one can pin you on anything. That's all that's important to him—not getting pinned."

Then there's Fred, the guy who is happy with surfaces. The one always moving to greener pastures. He's the mover, the person who likes to skim the cream off a relationship, or a book, or an idea, or a place. He likes the outside of things. It bores him to have to sit down and really talk to another person. He normally is busy, busy, busy and he intends to stay that way and the longer he stays that way the more he will need to stay that way. He dreads depth. He dreads being known. He's the guy on the psychiatrist's couch moaning, "Help me, Doc, my wife understands me."

Of course, his minister could *tell* Fred that his responsibility is to fill his own need for enlightenment, substance, and meaning. But if something is wrong with the thing inside Fred that "sees" those needs, so that he really believes that because he is rich he "has need of nothing," then of course his effect on other people will be destructive.

When a person has no awareness of his own needs, then anything he does for another is guilt-inducing. If you have no need for my help, then anything you do for me will obligate me to you. You will try to do what I ask only because *I* want or need it. This makes me feel guilty. It makes me feel there is something wrong with the fact that it's always *me* that needs response.

The one word that came to mind when I first met one acquaintance was "responsibility." Now I see she is stuck in her career. She feels she's a growing person because she's grown in her ability to handle her workload, make big advances in the income tax business she's in. I think, "Hey, that's great!" when she tells me of her achievements. I'm even beginning to think that maybe a person doesn't have to be growing in sensitivity, openness, insight in order to be a growing person.

Then her husband gallumphs into the room and starts to say something. She interrupts him. Corrects him. Not once. Not twice. But interruption and correction is her way of life. If he wants to say something, he finds he might as well settle for a discordant duet. Listening is so painful I have this awful urge to clap my hands over my ears and begin hollering, "Yah, yah, yah, yah, yahhhhhhhh," like I did when I was a mean little kid.

That isn't all. She begins to tell me in front of her husband (that's her husband over there looking a lot like a chicken, head drooped) that she *has* to work. That he is such a lousy provider ("Common laborers don't earn a heck of a lot, you know") that she has no choice. "But it's all just as well," she finishes. "I would never have grown if I hadn't been forced to work."

Also you can get stuck in faking response—I call it "charm." Charm is something you do, while responsive is something you are—and Rosie got stuck as a lot of southern women do, on acting "charmin'." Rosie could charm birds out of trees. She knows every method of getting her own way—from flattery to doormat submission to a new wardrobe of far-out clothes complete with headbands. But Rosie is fading out. At least her audience is. What Rosie really loved, her growing children and former friends have concluded, was not people. Rather, getting her own way.

I wouldn't really recommend Rosie's trap at all because it gets rough when people catch on. The opposite of responsive is materialistic, selfish, and manipulating—and when someone *really* catches onto your motive, that's the end of your act.

We were talking the other evening about the unpardonable sin, a group of us, and one of the guys said, "I don't know what God thinks is unforgivable, but I know what I find unforgivable. That's when you make the discovery that everything the person you really love wants out of life, or out of you, can be bought with dollar bills. Or when you find they prefer surfaces to reality. When they prefer the *appearance* of a good relationship to the *reality* of a good relationship because the reality requires something they don't want to give."

You can also confuse sex with responsiveness. There's my friend, Jen, who taught her daughter how to win a guy, helped stuff her wardrobe with chic and glamorous and sexy clothes. Taught her, by example, how to snuggle and coo and keep a clean house and at least feign an interest in her new husband and stomp her foot prettily to get what she wants. Jen has even made sure her daughter has "accepted Jesus," as she puts it — but Jen has forgotten that thing that Mary had — the ability to respond.

Her daughter, you see, is all but completely closed on any subject except herself. She never gets in touch with anyone unless she wants something. When her real self, which lurks an inch or so below the surface, begins to emerge, then her husband will either blame himself for this change in his once-lovely-acting wife, or the marriage will fail. If the marriage fails, it won't be the failure of knowledge about sex or sexy techniques and ways, but the failure always accompanying unresponsiveness.

While most of us are stuck in wanting our own ways and are at least ashamed enough of our condition to want to cover it, Harv, for example, blatantly wants his own way and believes fervently that anyone who isn't striving to be Number One has a gland missing or has skipped a stage in his development. Harv didn't really need to get to Frankfurt a few months ago, but in order to prove he can get anything he wants, he developed Instant Cancer so he could get the next flight to

Frankfurt, filled hours before. He finally got the best seat too. Harv is such a convincing liar he almost had the German ticket agent in tears (Harv was almost dead on the terminal floor), and the agent managed to shove someone else off the plane so Harv could get on.

A few friends are even stuck in "growing." Imagine *that*. A friend of a friend of a friend of mine says her husband is leaving her because he is growing and she is not. She says she can't see any perceptible growth unless it's for the paunch around his middle or the fact that he's definitely growing older or that he's growing his hair out in a new longer hairstyle for his young girl friend. So you can't just say "growth" anymore without someone thinking you mean the freedom to go braless or to live in a commune or to become a connoisseur of fine wine or to have more Holy Joe or Madame Goonsby experiences than anyone in town. This "growth" means developing your potential, though it might well be, as Socrates suggested, that one's potential may be to become a criminal.

Maybe one of the most boring traps to get stuck in is the trap of the well-planned goal-striver with his pockets bulging with lists. I fully suspect that in the story of the Good Samaritan at least two of the people who passed by on the other side were list-makers. Herb Gardner writes about a budding list-maker: "And he started to make lists this year. Lists of everything: subway stops, underwear, what he's gonna do next week. If somebody doesn't watch out he'll start making lists of what he's gonna do the next ten years. Hey . . . suppose they put him in with a whole family of list-makers? He'll learn to know everything before it happens, he'll learn how to be one of the nice dead people. . . ."

There are even nice respectable religious traps to substitute for response. This guy doesn't want to seem to need a relationship—his answer to all of life is "trust Jesus." He thinks that when the rich man came to Jesus and wanted to follow him without giving up the priority he'd obviously given to his money, Jesus simply patted him on his wallet and said, "All you need to do is trust me." This guy thinks that when the guy told Jesus he wanted to go home and wait for his father to die before he became a follower, Jesus very lovingly held his hand and whispered, "Say, George, you've got this all wrong. Don't worry about a thing. All you need to do is trust me. Do a good job at home, George. Do it for me."

I was overhearing a conversation between two women in the next booth in the Wienerwald, shortly after Jan left. I wasn't eavesdropping, really I wasn't. They both had voices like sailors and I didn't happen to have my sack of cottonballs with me.

"I don't feel needed anymore," one of the women was complaining. Her friend kept trying to reassure her. "Of course you are needed, of course you are needed," she said.

I was having this devious urge to say something. I wanted to say, "You're right. You aren't needed. You aren't needed anymore for what you want and demand to be needed for. For physical things. Your children don't need you to wash their hands, put them on the potty anymore. Your husband could have always ironed his shirts if it wouldn't have humiliated you, or if he had needed to. You aren't needed anymore to make your famous spaghetti sauce because Big Boy did one better. You aren't needed for angel food cake and doughnuts because Betty Crocker and Winchell's make them so much easier. You aren't needed for physical things and that's all that has ever mattered to you. You aren't needed to *do* anymore but to *be*. To respond."

Love isn't something you do. Or appear to do, or try to do. Or something you learn. Love has nothing to do with doing at all, but with a whole way of responding.

THE RESPONSIVE PERSON

While the ladies at the Wienerwald would have had a difficult time differentiating between love and doing, between being and doing, it seemed to be one of those self-evident truths to the people in Jesus' day. When Jesus performed all kinds of miracles, it's strange to me, who is used to our modern way of thinking, that they didn't run around asking each other, "Hey, what does this guy *do*? Does he pray conversationally or use 'thee' and 'thou'? And *you* there—you were close to him when he healed that guy—did you notice whether he touched the guy he healed on the right arm or the left one?"

What they *did* ask was, "What manner of man is this, that even the winds and waves obey his voice?" It was as if they knew without being told that an egotistical, self-centered materialist would have no power over the elements of nature.

Kids who haven't yet supressed the truth they instinctively know are also aware of the difference between being and behavior. A teen-ager I know is trying to break up with his girl friend. "See, what happened is that I told her I couldn't go with her anymore," he said. "She wondered why. And I blurted, 'It's just the way you are I can't take.' And she keeps asking what she's *done*, as if I can put a whole way of being selfish into a sentence like, 'Your arms are too skinny.'"

The emphasis on doing leads to self-righteousness. St. Paul equated the two: "Not of works, lest any man should boast," as if the belief that love is something you can win or work for, whether it's God's love or your husband's, is the very hub of self-righteousness. The real fact is that because there is a difference between the spirit (motive) in which I act and the action itself, I could be careful to never say one judgmental word about another person and yet be a very judgmental person.

"Judge not" doesn't refer to words and actions, but to the judgmental spirit. If you rave about people who criticize, if you control all conversations with your judgments of "that's being critical" or "you shouldn't say that," then your main problem is itself a critical spirit, a response problem, even though you may never *say* a critical word. (Looking at your watch anxiously says, "Hurry up and finish your sentence." Kicking your child's wagon across the yard says, "Why are you so messy?")

You'd almost think Jesus was advocating love as something you do rather than a way of responding. But then you realize that everything he commanded was something you have to *be* before you can do it. Like when he told the rich man to sell all he had, he was telling him what he had to *be*—spiritual and perceptive enough to prefer joy that was free and not dependent on anything.

St. Paul described love as a certain way of being or responding when he said, "Love is not arrogant." He didn't say—not ever—"Try to act less arrogant, and as you act less arrogant you will become more and more loving." Which is exactly the belief of the person who puts doing before responding.

He said you could give your body to be burned, give away your new house, furniture, long johns, have all kinds of things—knowledge, praise-the-Lord experiences, pots of gold—but if you aren't a certain kind of person you're still a Big Zero. "Nothing" is how Paul put it.

He says love endures long and is patient and kind. It never is envious or jealous or boastful or overconfident or exhibitionistic. All the while it is very clear that you can't possibly go at it the other way around; you can't acquire the habit of acting less jealous and think you are more loving. You can't give your last mite to feed the poor, give your body to be burned, or speak in tongues and connect it in any way with love, because you can have all the forms of love and yet deny or reject that state of being that motivates loving actions.

What really has amazed me about the early believers was

their ability to simplify the most profound truths; it's as if they inherited the trait from Jesus. If you would have asked Jesus about growth or the nature of response or what allows growth to happen or what it is that grows from seed to full-blown insight, he would probably sit down and motion for you to sit down too, and like any really terrific teacher he would satisfy your need to understand by tossing you an image to play with. It would be an image so fantastic that once your subconscious internalized it and allowed it to germinate and send out roots deep into your heart's understanding, it would keep making all kinds of new connections in your thinking. And like the mustard seed that begins as the tiniest of seeds and keeps on reproducing, this word or image would keep on producing and reproducing new insights in you the rest of your life.

Jesus pictured four qualities of response (response and personality are almost synonymous terms) in his parable of four soils. When you let those images really soak in, pretty soon you begin to see a lot of things you never saw before.

The first type of soil he described, the wayside soil, looks to me like an example of passivity. Such a person (soil) feels no need or responsibility to search for the meaning of the message he is given, no need to understand or grasp or comprehend even the most elementary principles governing life. Life just happens to him. He is acted *upon*. He takes no responsibility for his emotional thought-life. It doesn't occur to him to search beneath fear for the thought that produced that fear, or to search beneath misbehavior for its motive, because the truly irresponsible person is always a believer in the lie that everything is caused by his environment. This is why all his energies are consumed with excuses, rationalizations, reasons, and blaming.

If you've known him very long, you know this person is the master of the predictable response ("Do you want sugar in your tea?" "No, I'm sweet enough, thank you." "How about lemon?" "I like lemon, but lemon doesn't like me.") His language betrays his irresponsibility and passivity. (He didn't break the eggs. The eggs became broken. He didn't frustrate his child. His child got angry.)

Rollo May writes in *Existential Psychology*, "We can demonstrate at every moment of the day in our psychotherapeutic work that only the truth that comes alive more than an abstract idea and is 'felt on the pulse' . . . only this truth has the power to change a human being." There's a close connection between that statement and this scriptural indictment: "While any one is hearing the Word of the kingdom and does not grasp and comprehend it, the evil one comes and snatches away what is sown in his heart. This is what was sown along the roadside."

The second picture is that of the shallow soil. This is the shallow person who receives the message "with great joy" but is unproductive. Response is initially a positive attraction, not subject to my conscious will (similar in this way to romantic love). This positive attraction comes as a feeling to some, but Jesus hints that it isn't the *feeling* that is productive, but the communing, relating, back-and-forth tension of response which bears fruit and which is the essence of all true creativity. This truth is verified in any number of places. ("As for what was sown on the good soil, this is he who hears the Word and grasps and comprehends it. He indeed bears fruit." Or, as Rollo May would put it, this truth that comes alive, the truth that is "seen" and understood, has the power to change a human being.)

The Old Testament states the same principle: "He that meditates day and night will be like a tree planted by the rivers of water . . . and everything he doeth will prosper." This "meditating day and night" can only be referring to the subconscious heart processes that never sleep. The "heart" responds to ideas. It is not aware of its own responses or its own beliefs—it is the part in me that believes or responds in a certain way *before* my conscious self is aware of what it believes or responds to. "As a man thinks in his heart so is he," helps me realize that it is this spontaneous heart response that determines my reactions as well as my actions.

The shallow person is one whose response is a giddy feeling, whose heart does not care to cope with the dimension of patterns and ideas and images, whose life is subject to external circumstances. This person has no roots and no depth.

The third image in the parable is this picture of the thorny soil. While the shallow person can be done in by the bad times, this guy is done in by the good times. The soil earlier given to the Word is now given to "cares and riches." He becomes unproductive; the thoughts he has internalized never develop into personal conviction, awareness, virtue as he continues to lose interest in the ideas and convictions that shape his life.

The fourth image is the "good soil." Carl Rogers writes that the growing, maturing person is in process. As he puts it: "Being a process is positively valued. From desiring some fixed goal, clients come to prefer the excitement of being a process." Response is neither a feeling nor a behavior, but response implies an object to respond to and is therefore an *inner* relationship between soil and seed, responder and message responded to . . . and this response is not a decision or an act of the will, but a process involving listening to the message, absorbing, struggling with the message, talking to it, asking it questions, allowing it to reveal itself to you, to develop into wisdom.

Jesus called this process "the work of believing," but some today would refer to it as "the creative process." It is not a conscious work or process requiring high intelligence or hard thinking, but rather faith. You simply give room and attention to it because you know it to have great importance.

To respond in and from the heart is to search for the *meaning* of the message that comes to you, with no ulterior motive except to understand. One person explains the process: "I had been noticing that once I heard a message that I felt had great meaning and importance if I could only understand it, and would take it into myself, I found I could be absorbed in my housework or taking care of the children and yet beneath all this, in what seemed to be the depth of me somewhere, was a place where ideas and images would develop into rare and beautiful thoughts that had never occurred to me before—new interpretations of old truth—and when I would share those interpretations and thoughts with others they were always new to the person I shared them with too. I found that I had to allow the message to think in me without telling it what it had to think according to popular theology or in order not to be considered a heretic."

I like Erich Fromm's description of responsive persons: ". . . those who approach a situation by preparing nothing in advance, not bolstering themselves up in any way. Instead they respond spontaneously and productively. They forget about themselves, about the knowledge, the positions they have. . . .

"Their egos do not stand in their own way, and it is precisely for this reason that they can fully respond to the other person and that person's idea.

"They give birth to new ideas because they are not holding onto anything and can thus produce and give. . . .

"They come fully alive in conversation, because they do not stifle themselves by anxious concern with what they have.

"Their own aliveness is infectious and often helps the other person to transcend his or her egocentricity. Thus the conversation ceases to be an exchange of commodities (information, knowledge, status) and becomes a dialogue in which it does not matter any more who is right."

While response is a living, breathing, laughing, crying, spontaneous, back-and-forth, graceful, flowing connectedness, the opposite of response is self-awareness, self-centeredness, and all the forms of materialism—hanging on, displaying, performing, possessing, and refusing to let go.

When I was a little girl I had a friend who would invite me over to her house to play dolls with her. I would drag my only doll with me and while I would talk and croon and rock and diaper my doll, she would line her dolls up on a shelf, display them, and categorize them. I really wouldn't have been surprised if she had had a card catalogue with a card filed on each of them, complete with their vital statistics.

I found the same principle as an adult. Sometimes I think I've found someone I can share this inner dialogue with—someone to walk on the water with me (no need to have memorized answers or solid orthodox ground beneath me every moment)—and I'll look up and realize that this person has a fragile ego that I must constantly stop and nurse, and so any new connections and all those gorgeous insights go unconnected and unseen. Dan says it's been the same with him. There he is with his tongue hanging out, working out some exhausting problem, and Wilbur will saunter into his office, biting the stems of his glasses and being so concerned with appearing concerned that he has no time to be concerned. So Dan sees wearily that he goes it alone or not at all.

The old prophets bawled (probably very unprettily) on the street corners that the reason the people were unresponsive (had eyes that couldn't see and ears that couldn't hear) was materialism—the worship of their own achievements and good works and all that is involved in "the works of man's hands." Materialism was known then to be "the root of all evil," the cause of apathy, deadness, flatness, stagnation, rigidity, loss of soul, identity, uniqueness, etc.

But since materialism has very little to do with money, and everything to do with ways of thinking and seeing, *that*, gentle reader (as Elsie Dinsmore said), is what we want to talk about.

FOUR
THE ACHIEVER

Overcoming materialistic attitudes isn't easy. You can't seek to be a kind, sweet, loving person as an end in itself; you can only seek God. But we have to begin somewhere. A good place to start is in the junk pile of ego-traps, clearing away the evasions and excuses that push love away.

We have already seen examples of these substitutes for love—these ego-traps. Remember my little friend next door who described his uncle this way?: "That's all that's important to him—not getting pinned." This is the ego-trap of defensiveness or self-protection.

Then there was Fred, who was afraid of going deeper than the surface ("Help me, Doc, my wife understands me"). And there's the career ego-trap that Rhoda fell into, prizing her advancement in life over her own husband. There was charmin' Rosie who mastered the ego-trap of manipulation, and Jen who taught her daughter the ego-trap of sexiness. There was the perpetual list-maker who makes an ego-trap out of planning to do things.

Harv too, you'll remember, was stuck in an ego-trap. The Me Mentality. Harv blatantly deified his self, and he believed fervently that anyone who doesn't strive to be *numero uno* has a gland missing or something. To get where he wanted to be he developed Instant Cancer to get on the plane.

In spite of the fantastic number and variety of ego-traps, my awareness of only one or two (people-pleasing, for example) limits me in dealing with these excuses for love.

But what I really want to get down to in this chapter is Murielism. . . .

Muriel is forty-five. Pretty. Slim. Fashionable haircut. Streaked hair. Muriel is attractive. Very attractive.

Muriel is a doer. A go-getter. A woman of many—well, I started to say occupations, but actually I guess I mean *preoccupations*. To Muriel, achievement is very, very important. Accomplishment. Doing. The type of person who can't enjoy a trip to the Alps unless she can teach the mountain people how to decorate bathrooms.

Lists as long as telephone wires lie around the house. "Check, check, yes, that's done. Yes, that too. Check, check. And you, my dear? Where can I fit you in? Here, I know, I'll put you right here—this fifteen minutes while the fluffables are fluffing in the drier."

(My friend Barb is going with a male version of Muriel. Barb is in her late twenties, still dating, and one thing that drives her crazy, she says, is that most German men want to relegate her to one evening of the week. Monday is for this. Tuesday for that. Wednesday, the soccer game on television. Friday, the evening with the guys, playing cards. Saturday evening with his parents. Sunday afternoon, walks in the park. Barb gets Thursday.

"The last guy I met had a look in his eyes that said, 'You would fit so neatly into my Thursday evening slot between 7:00 and 10:30,'" Barb laughs. "And as long as I would let him fit me into that little slot, as long as I didn't suggest I'd like to see him on Friday night too, everything would be okay.")

Muriel is also a good daughter. She and Mamma can talk forty-five minutes on the telephone about what kind of halter dress Prissy should wear to the school dance. And Muriel is never one to neglect her family—she is a wonderful cook. What meals! What omelettes! The only woman I've ever known who could stuff snails.

They tell us there are two basic kinds of people—the My Way person and the Your Way person. Muriel is a My Way person. There is one way to wash dishes ("Here, they must be stacked to the left of the sink after rinsing, glasses first, silverware over here"), there is one way to eat a breakfast roll ("You cut it in two—this way—lengthwise is the best way"), and there is one way to spread jam ("Grape is best. It spreads much easier. It's especially better than currant jelly, which has all those bumpy currants").

Muriel sees love as something you work for—and therefore an achievement. She works very hard for love. She does not, cannot see herself as the recipient of love, the receiver of love, but always Muriel is the *cause* of love. Does Charlie love her? It cannot be because of some goodness in Charlie. It cannot be because of the nature of love itself. It has *got* to be something Muriel has done. And done perfectly.

Does Charlie give her gifts? The reason is (don't tell anyone), but the real reason is because Muriel is so appreciative.

Is Charlie successful in his work? The reason (shhhh, quiet now, sweetheart, Muriel wouldn't want to take all the credit, you know), the reason is really because Muriel is such a wonderful hostess. Because Muriel delights her family and friends with food outrageously tempting. Because Muriel is so dynamic. Because Muriel can throw the grandest parties. Couples come in twos to Muriel's parties. Like Noah's Ark. People are not really people to Muriel, but "couples." Muriel loves to entertain *couples*; and if you are not a part of a successful and delightful couple, you—well, I don't want to hurt your feelings, dahling, but you wouldn't be visible. You just wouldn't exist to Muriel. Muriel could look right at you, look right through you, wouldn't know you were there.

Muriel is a good wife, if good means protective. Just as Muriel has protective glass on her desk, Scotch tape on the corners of gilt frames to keep them chip-free, she also protects Charlie. She has always needed to be Right. Always needed to be Best. Now, since Charlie is hers, since Charlie belongs to her, it is nearly as satisfying for Charlie to be Right. For Charlie to be Best.

Muriel not only loves work, doing, achievement—she also seems to love people. But you would almost get the idea that Muriel regards people as possessions. As pieces of property. To be referred to as "mine." My hubby. My doctor. My dentist. My friend. My pastor. My children. My Randall. (Of course there is also my diet, my operation, my medication, my yogurt recipe, my prayers, my idea.)

Muriel's children are achievers. All but one. The one who is not (her name is Pam)—well, Muriel is still trying. And praying for her. Guiding her by constant reminders. Oh, not nagging, of course. Muriel hates nagging. Just caring, thoughtful compliments about Pam's friends. How beautiful Gracie is! What lovely posture Janet has! How stunning Marcie looks in her clothes! How proud Ann must make her parents, bringing home straight A's and all! And as for Pam's attitudes—I've noticed that Pam is unselfish and generous— well, Muriel never really notices them; she never cared much about her children's attitudes. I mean, really now, what could you *do* with a lovely attitude? Put it on the mantle? Frame it? Come on, now—let's be realistic.

Muriel is a trifle indecisive. Choices are hard for her, not because she is a woman (as she has convinced her husband), but because how she looks is terrifically important to her. (Muriel wouldn't want people to think she is a *slob*, you know.) What shoes will Muriel wear with this little black dress? Black? That's it. The black ones. The ones with the strap. No, the ones with the open toe. No, beige would be ever so much better with the beige trim on the dress. Oh no, the black. Oh dear, it better be the beige.

Muriel's actions spring, of course, from her heart. From her values. Muriel values perfection and work as the way to perfection. Muriel knows you are going to love her more if she becomes more perfect. If she never gets tired. If she never needs to go to the john on a trip.

Muriel is a certain kind of Christian. The kind of Christian who finds faith in God a kind of fun thing—a kind of Spiritual Amusement in which one arranges certain accepted formulas into neat mental arrangements without bothering to wonder what anything means, or to care whether it means anything at all.

Understanding is very low on Muriel's hierarchy of values. Muriel believes there is no need to wonder about the way things are. About reality. No need to ask questions in this life. When we get to heaven God will explain everything we have never wondered about. Those things we never cared to know.

I can see it now—all of us sitting in a Group Meeting in heaven. That's Muriel over there. Her robe is spotless. She has soaked her crown in ammonia all afternoon—(see it sparkle!). She has just introduced God to all of us. She has just made a clever little joke and now she is turning to God. "Now, God," she says, "we ladies would appreciate it if you would limit your explanation of the Mysteries of the Ages to fifteen minutes. We have prepared the coffee and Hot Frippies, and we wouldn't want them to get cold, now would we, God?"

THE ACHIEVER

To Muriel, faith does not mean letting go of the world and holding onto God. Faith to Muriel, as all things are, is something you *do*. She finds she can work faith in most conveniently between 8:00 and 8:30 in the morning as the moisturizer slithers into her astringent-clean face. Everyone has left the house for the day and now she has time for faith, time to picture the things she wants to happen that she hasn't accomplished yet by hard work. But picturing positively can be hard work too—especially when the skin specialist doesn't allow you to wrinkle your brow. Muriel is now picturing positively, by which she means picturing Prissy marrying a doctor. Or Charlie Junior giving the opening address at the American Medical Association. Oh yes, whatever happens, however rushed Muriel is, she will find time for faith.

"Hey, Muriel," I ask once, "ever think about Jonah?"

"Jonah Who?" Muriel asks.

"You know—Jonah and the Whale," I remind her.

"Oooooooo!" Muriel titters in controlled merriment. "I thought you meant Jonah Livingston. Did you hear what happened to his daughter?"

"No, Muriel—I mean Jonah and the Whale. Did you ever think about how God saved all the people of Nineveh through Jonah? How God does no mighty works where there is unbelief? And yet Jonah didn't picture positively. He came out of the whale shrunken to half his size, stinking clear to the next town, not a hair on his head, seaweed hanging out of his teeth, hoping the horrible Ninevites wouldn't repent, and yet God worked through him anyway to save a whole city."

"Oooooooo," Muriel moans. "Can't we talk about something positive? Negative thinking makes me sick. Literally *sick*." (Negative thinking to Muriel is any conversation in which she is not in control.)

To Muriel, everything is simple. Everything is either. Or it is or. You are either all good, in which case your telephone will never be silent, your mailbox never empty. Or you are all bad, in which case Muriel won't be able to recognize you in the local IGA. This simplicity comes from the fact that, to Muriel, good is the opposite of bad. She has elevated bad not by proclaiming it to be a pathetic parasite on the Tree of Good, but by declaring it the opposite of good. Good and bad are two things in the external world, so this simplifies things even further for Muriel. There is no reason to wonder about the root of action, about motivations, values, attitudes. She resents such complications intruding into her black and white, clear-cut conception of herself and others.

I haven't decided if it's perfection and hard work Muriel loves, or reality she hates. Anyway, Muriel wants things to work. Something is *true* if it works. The Bible is true if it works. You think there is something wrong with her pragmatic philosophy and she answers, "Well, it works doesn't it?" If it works to give her what she wants, that is Truth for Muriel.

Ask Muriel some desperate burning question about life and existence (because Muriel is an adult Sunday school teacher) and Muriel will murmur as she snuggles even closer to Charlie, "Oh, I'm sorry I'm so dumb. I'm so dumb, aren't I, Charlie? Charlie is the one with the brains in the house," and Charlie, forgetting the desperate question (as Muriel has planned), will come to Muriel's defense, as surely as if Muriel had been attacked. Muriel has poked the Absolutely Right Button once again.

Yes, it's true. Muriel has a most difficult time forgetting herself. The answer is always "Yes, but." Yes, but what about me? Yes, but where do I come into this? Yes, but how do you think that makes me feel?

Now, Muriel's body is terribly important to her. She knows every verse in the Bible about her body being the temple of the Holy Ghost. Muriel wants the Holy Ghost to have a nice house to live in, so she jogs every day. She has a wardrobe for jogging. Little blue and white jogger's togs, white tennies, blue and white headband — the whole works. It is very important to Charlie, Muriel reminds me, that she have a lovely body.

Work helps Muriel. Keeps her from having to face herself. Her day is planned around it so nothing spontaneous will happen to frighten her or throw her day off.

"You must have a schedule," she tells me, "or you cannot get your work done."

"I don't have a schedule, Muriel, and yet I get my work done."

"But you can't," Muriel says.

"But I do, Muriel."

"But you can't," Muriel lectures me. "You can't get things done without a schedule. You just can't. Can't brush your teeth, get breakfast, get the kids out the door without a schedule."

"I don't brush my teeth just because it's 7:00," I say. "I brush them because I hate fur on my teeth. I don't make breakfast just because it's 7:10, but because we're hungry." Trying to explain that was as difficult as explaining to a small child what the day before yesterday means.

The day before coming back to the States, I attend a study group with Muriel. The teacher suggests that when we get to heaven we are going to find little piles all over heaven — one for each person — things God had wanted to send down to us when we were on earth, but which he couldn't send because we hadn't asked for them. While I am trying to recover from my embarrassment at such non-thinking, I feel a jab in the rib with a sharp elbow. Muriel is smiling. Muriel likes that idea. What does Muriel picture on her "pile"? A rich husband for Prissy? A houseful of new shag carpeting so deep you could trip in it? Whatever it is, I'm sure Muriel now is going to ask for it.

Did you ever read *The Stepford Wives*? It's a story about a whole town of Muriels. A whole town of men who want to be left alone — married to women like Muriel who keep so busy they are glad to leave their husbands alone. The book starts out kinda cute. Two real, warm, funny women and their husbands move into this town peopled entirely with perfectionist men who love perfectionist women. Like I say, it's kinda cute and funny. And then, without warning, an icy hand reaches in and snatches your heart, scares you to death. Please God, you think, please don't let those men do what I think they are going to do to those two normal women. Perfectionism isn't evil. Is it, God, is it? Oh yes, it is. It *is*. Perfectionism and Murielism wouldn't do that, would they, God? Wouldn't turn those warm, funny, human women into some kind of Awful Robots? It's a real chiller-killer, that's what.

Well, do you see how Muriel, the Achiever, has become a perfectionist? It's easy to do. The person who values doing may come to value *having done*, and then having things done *right*. It's a subtle shift, but it is a shift, and it leads us to examine another ego-trap. Idealism.

FIVE
THE IDEALIST

Goldy is an Idealist whose life is completely governed by "shoulds." She's currently distraught with her child. "He hurries home from school. Sticks his nose in a book. Doesn't ever bring a friend home."

"Hey," I say, "what kind of books does he read?"

"Who cares? He should bring his friends home from school. There's something wrong with a person who won't bring his friends home from school."

"Maybe he's sick of looking at those kids by the time school is over — maybe he's got terrific interests."

"I don't care," Goldy interrupts coldly. "A kid who doesn't bring his friends home from school isn't normal. He should. That's all." And so she continues to nag him. She has no interest in knowing the child she is raising.

The Idealist's talk is always somewhere else. He is thinking about what or whom he is trying to work on, change, or make over. What he is actually doing is rejecting. Rejecting anything that exists in favor of what should exist.

The Idealist will admire you when you are thinner. He will be happy when he retires in Arizona. His goal is never an inner goal (to change his own reactions and responses to his environment—to admire you even if you are ten pounds overweight, or to be happy even if he is in the Army), but an external goal—to get you thin. (Of course, when you do get thin, his mind will have already jumped ahead to something else he has discovered to be the cause of his unhappiness with you—that chipped tooth? How about your right foot, slightly shorter than the left?)

An elderly widower is an idealist. He is describing the kind of woman he is looking for. Young (around twenty-five years old), long, swinging hair, tall, slim, a figure like this (he lifts his eyebrows in ooh-la-la fashion, putting his briefcase down so he can draw a figure in the air for us with both hands).

My neighbor's sister, who is visiting, finally had enough. "Tell you what I'll do, George," she said in a tone that felt like ice cubes. "Tell you what—it sounds like the kind of chick you want could be found at the University, so I'll put up a sign in Taylor Hall for you—something like this: 'Baldheaded, paunchy, fiftyish man wants girl with long, swingy hair, 5'8" tall, measurements 36-23-36.'"

We all laughed together and George, being good-natured, laughed right along with us. Maybe we all realized together for one split-second that idealism can make a person eternally out-of-date. Hopelessly stuck. The Jews bowed to golden calves—we bow to Goldie Hawns, perpetual springtimes, and eternal youth. (Wasn't it Lewis who said, "All that is not eternal is eternally out of date"?)

The Idealist sees perfection as something tangible. Adolph Hitler, who had all handicapped people done away with, was one. The Idealist who won't allow the intrusion of reality into his fantasies will eventually, strangely enough, reject the ultimate perfection, God himself. Abraham Maslow writes of a subject who "lost her religion because she simply could not believe in a God who had invented such a nasty, dirty, disgusting way of making babies."

There are many forms of idealism. There are the positive thinkers who believe they can change reality by picturing what they want to happen, and so they spend their energies on dreaming rather than on discovering. They believe that you can manufacture reality by "believing" hard enough so what isn't so becomes so. It doesn't really matter what you *are*. What you *think* you are is what is important.

"The reason Muhammad Ali is the champ is because he thinks he is," one of these positive thinkers said recently.

"That's not positive thinking," I tease. "It would never even pass for *thinking*. Maybe the reason the champ thinks he is, is because he is. If he weighed ninety pounds, couldn't beat his way out of a wet paper sack, and still thought he was the champ, you'd think he was a *nut*, not a champ." Seems to me that what I am and what I think I am must be very similar in order for me to be an honest, realistic person.

Idealism is devious in its approach. I go to write in a cafe. What I really want this morning is something with my coffee. One of those French croissants in the window I saw as I walked in. I know I have to say no to that whim, so I just order coffee. And soon I begin to see how absolutely devious this should-self is.

"Hey, look," it begins to reason with me, "you sit at this table for at least two hours. You take all that space—and really you ought to order more than a pot of coffee. You ought to order at least a breakfast roll."

I don't catch on for a moment. "Okay, maybe so."

"How about that French roll you saw as you came in?"

Now I see what I'm doing. I'm changing "I want" to "I should" so I don't have to feel guilty and so I can talk myself into getting what I want. "I want" is something I must take responsibility for (that's why irresponsible people very seldom use the phrase). "I should," on the other hand, puts the responsibility for my action *outside* myself. If you follow the inner dialogue closely, you can see how "should" thinking not only leads to irresponsibility, but it also leads to self-righteousness. (The reason I'm ordering the roll is that I don't feel I am being fair *not* ordering a roll.)

Failure to grow away from shoulds, idealism, and goal-striving leads to a whole lifetime of self-condemnation, rather than self-understanding.

I used to believe, for example, that messiness or disorganization was not only inconvenient and sometimes frustrating—but I actually believed it to be *wrong*. Sinful. By messiness, maybe I should explain that I don't mean dirty hair. A greasy sink. Yukky rings in the bathtub. Leaving messes other people had to clean up in order to survive. Berdyaev, the philosopher, might have termed what I'm referring to more politely as "the dark, meonic freedom."

So I go on duty to become a neat person. That's my goal—to become a neat person. I criticize myself. Tear myself apart. Tell myself how super-bad I am to be so messy. After all, I don't exist in a certain way, do I? No, I'm a blank sheet of paper on which everyone writes.

I can become my ideal, right? I can do anything, be anything I want to be. I can be anti-messy if I try. I am boss over this messy, disorganized self. I am in control, right?

Wrong. I begin to notice something. As soon as my critical self goes off duty, as soon as this critical, idealistic self stops bossing my behavior around, this other self that exists in a certain way not subject to change goes right back to being disorganized. Harem-scarem.

So I keep on constant duty, consume huge gulps of energy, get up from my nap and start in with another sermon. "Shame on you for being messy. Shape up or ship out." I am the Critic. The Judge. The Examiner. The Analyzer. I can't imagine at this point simply observing my behavior to see what it's trying to tell me.

But one day I see something—this bossing and preaching and idealizing isn't doing even a tiny bit of good. I see it is self-defeating. I find that the first step in loving myself is becoming aware that there exists in myself real needs that need to be met, real interests that need to be pursued, and real questions that need to be answered.

I learn some good first lessons about this absolute self in me. That this self that manifests itself through my body and behavior doesn't very often measure up to what the world calls "good." I want this self (I'll refer to it as Me) to measure up—but Me cares nothing at all about measuring up. Me only cares about being. About being what it is. About being real. Me cares nothing at all about conforming. Me seems only to want to be known by this other self. To be visible to this other self. To be understood by this other self.

I begin to become aware that I am two kinds of Me. I am the person who is. Who exists in a certain way. The person who wants to be known. I am also the person who finally, at long last, wants to understand, know, and love, rather than to change and shape and form.

I am what I am. I am also what I think I am. I want these two people to become united, to like each other. Most of my problems come from the separation of my heart (what I am) and my head (what I think I am).

"Why are you so messy?" I ask Me (rather than "shame on you for being so messy!"). "Don't you care about order?"

"Maybe," Me says, after a while. "I don't care a lot about order as you understand order."

I am amazed. Maybe I am going to have to relearn from Me what order is all about. It is clear that Me doesn't care about order as I had always understood order. Maybe if I listen very carefully to this knower in me that understands inner (rather than outer) things I can find out a lot of things I didn't know before.

But now I am eighteen, and at this time I would rather listen to the people around me I consider in-the-know, rather than to Me. See—there I am over there—packing my suitcase for choir tour. I am to room ("Please God, help my roommate") with a Neat Person. A thoroughly Neat Person. The Neat Person's name is Frances.

One bright morning while I am still rubbing my eyes, Neat Person who has been wide-awake and singing "Ah, Sweet Mystery of Life" since 5:00 says, "I don't like the way you pack your suitcase."

I laugh (that's me over there on the bed, laughing like a madman). "Yeah, it is kind of awful, isn't it, Frances?"

Frances isn't laughing. In fact, I don't remember ever seeing Frances laugh. She is folding my slips and bras. She is folding a blue nightgown carefully and neatly for me.

I stop her. I feel guilty. "Hey," I say, "is there something wrong? I mean, really now, is there something really bad about a sloppy suitcase?"

Neat Person blinks her baby blue eyes. "It's very inconvenient for you," she says.

"I don't mind," I say. "I fold my sweaters. I make sure my skirts don't wrinkle, but I really don't mind having wrinkled underwear. I really don't."

"But you really should be neat," Frances says.

"Yeah, I'm sure you're right," I grudgingly admit.

"I mean, you can't know where anything is," Frances urges, feeling that my sense of guilt is reaching a climax.

"Sure I do," I disagree. "I have a photographic memory. Is that okay?"

"No." Frances laughs nervously. "It's really not. The fact is that it's so much easier to keep things neat."

"Easier for whom?" I want to know.

"Easier for everyone. Ask anyone. They'll tell you it's easier."

"I'll find anyone and ask her tomorrow. Right now I'd like

to go back to sleep," I yawn rudely. "I really, at this moment, don't see any sense in arranging my underwear alphabetically. I find that my way saves time for me."

"Well, it's not right," she finally says. "It's simply not right. It's not good to be messy. You know that. Everyone knows that."

A light turns on in my head. I was not a Christian at this time as Frances was, but I had grown up in a home where I had learned the Bible and I found myself, unconsciously at first, measuring all of this against the Bible. Were there any such shoulds in the Bible? Did the Bible say anything at all about messiness? "Hey, cool it, Frances," I finally say, sitting bolt upright in bed. "You're making a moral issue out of neatness. You really are. And the way I pack my suitcase simply isn't a moral issue."

Frances blinks. She looks as if no one has ever questioned her judgments.

"It really isn't," I repeat, just seeing this for myself. "Order is important. But maybe that doesn't mean order like order. Maybe there's inner order and outer order. Maybe inner order has something to do with 'in order of importance.'"

"Why do you have to start getting intellectual about something as simple as the way you pack a suitcase?" Frances complains.

"Look, Frances, you started it. As I was saying, maybe order of importance might mean that it's more important to be messy and un-nosy as to be neat and condemning. Maybe it has something to do with a *lot* more than just being an Old Maid."

"Why do you have to make comments about Old Maids?" Frances asks, defensive as usual. Frances is huffy. That's Frances, banging out the door. Headed somewhere. Anywhere. Whew, maybe Frances is gone. No, Frances is poking her head in the door again. "I don't know why you have to doubt everything any normal person knows," she says, hoping it will be the last word on the subject.

"Listen, Frances," I say, "you want me to believe neatness is a moral issue because you say it is. You want me to believe in God because you tell me to. If my loyalty to God isn't based on my faith, my insight into how good he is—which it isn't at this point—then *saying* I believe means nothing anyway."

"You make me sick," Frances says, baring her pearly white teeth. "You'll never find God. Never in a thousand years."

One day after this, after I had temporarily suspended sentence on Me, a friend comes running over to the dorm, very excited. There is something she wants me to read. No, she doesn't trust me. She is going to read it *to* me.

She kicks her shoes off, makes a lunge for the bed, and opens the book. "There's a description, an exact description of you in this book," she pants. "I've got to read you this . . . and this. And this. . . ." And so she proceeds to read to me.

I listen in disbelief. The *very* traits I had hated most in myself were some of the traits Maslow lists as traits belonging to the self-actualizer—traits not good or bad in themselves, but all a part of a very intricate balanced pattern, as delicate as the body's hormonal balance. My image of the Perfect Self died at that moment and has never been resurrected.

By beginning to refuse to judge myself by the world's standards of shoulds and musts (and very often, the Church's standards of shoulds and musts), I begin to understand myself and *like* myself. It occurred to me, for example, that I wasn't messy and haphazard about everything—only about things I considered slightly trivial. When it came to things I considered important, I wouldn't tolerate fuzziness or messiness or inaccuracies. I would begin to wonder about a certain concept or principle and would leave nothing unturned until I found the answer that satisfied, until this responder-to-the-truth-in-me would jump up, clap her hands, and squeal with delight, "Hey, that's right! That's good! Really good!"

I found out later that I was not only being manipulated by shoulds. I was also manipulating by shoulds. That's me, over there, reading the story of Jacob and Esau to two little boys—that God loved Jacob and hated Esau.

"God shouldn't hate," a small voice pipes up. "You won't let us hate."

"You're right," I agree weakly. "God shouldn't hate. He also shouldn't have preferences. Maybe this was translated wrong or something." And so I let it drop. For a few minutes. Later on that evening I talked at God. Snow was falling outdoors. I stood at the window, watching it for a while, and then gave God proper warning of my wrath, "Now listen, God," I lecture sternly, "you tell me not to hate. And then you hate. You shouldn't do that. That's not nice. It's embarrassing—always having to explain your behavior to those kids. I can't love a God who hates arrogant people and loves humble people. A God who hates evil and loves good. It's simply not right."

Being through with my address, I blow my nose and stare out the window.

"Hey," the thought nudges me, "remember Frances?"

"Who would forget Frances?" I ask the thought.

"Quit being Frances. Allow God to be God rather than making God into an idol—a cold, rigid image of the kind of being you think he ought to be. Do you want to change God or understand what he's like?"

"Understand him, of course."

"If you want to understand, then you have to approach with humility and wonder—that's what 'the fear of God is the beginning of wisdom' is all about. Fear in the sense of awe. You have to allow your image of the perfect God to be shattered. God doesn't reveal himself to the know-it-all who prefers his own image of God to the real thing. . . .

"Give up your way. How you 'know' things are. Who you think God is. Let reality flow in on you. Have it's own way. Let it be. Be whatever it wants to be. Let it be itself. This is to be the meaning of your life—to understand. Not to change. . . ."

"Okay, God, be yourself. Maybe someday I can even approve of you being yourself."

I was remembering how I had felt only a few days before when I had resented exactly the same thing I was putting on God. When a person has a set image of me, even if he adores that image, I have this perverse desire to take that false image and smash it to the ground in a thousand pieces, as God wanted to smash the stupid idols men made of him. I had wanted to shock that person or yell, "Look at *me*, not that silly image of me. Maybe you'd prefer me to the image if you'd just look."

I have to give up my images, "cast down imaginations," before I can really grow. This image I make of myself gets created and pretty soon this image begins to tell me what I can do and can't do, starts to limit me and hold me in. This image gets in control and I am in for stagnation, and all the frightening things that spell death.

Christianity promises union with God, but before union can begin to occur, I have to go beyond shoulds, beyond condemnation, and break out of it as a butterfly breaks out of its cocoon. Just as the person incapable of giving up his boundaries, giving up the concept of "yours" and "mine" in favor of "ours" can never be married (even though he has been legally married), so I can only enter into the relationship with God by counting the cost, to see if I'm able to give up my idealism. My idols. My shoulds.

I'm thinking of the parable of the prodigal son. There he stands, the older brother, scolding his father because he has not behaved as he thinks he should. His father hasn't killed a fatted calf for him, but for his brother. And the father turns to him and says, "Son, everything I had was always yours." It was always so on the part of the father. What the father owned belonged to the son and always had. It was the *son* who perceived boundaries between what the father had and what he wanted.

Why did he perceive boundaries? Boundaries that weren't there? Why, sure, I see it now. It was because he wanted to keep some things for himself. Because he would rather have the few rags he considered his own than to share all the wealth in the world and give up the concept of "mine" forever. *That* was what the secretive, defensive brother couldn't stand.

To give up "mine" would mean to give up his self-righteousness (he would never again be able to see himself as "serving" the father). I mean, really now, how can you give the father what is already his? How can you serve the father by taking care of your things—things just as much yours as his?

But you see how this business of idealism is very tricky. Seductive. We start with shoulds and oughts; we wind up with laws and rules. And suddenly we've plunged deep into the pit of legalism.

SIX
THE LEGALIST

Dan applied for work at a Christian camp not many years ago. Mr. Snodgrass took his application. Know what Mr. Snodgrass wanted to know? What he thought was important? He wanted to know if Dan went to movies. He wanted to know if he drank beer. He wanted to know if he smoked cigarettes.

Mr. Snodgrass is a legalist to whom the most important thing is obedience to rules. Actually, he's concerned with *not* doing. He wouldn't have even thought of being concerned with anything as positive as depth of understanding (he would have been *positively* threatened by it). He wouldn't have even wondered about realness or recognized hypocrisy, being careful not to turn off those super-perceptive kids. He wouldn't have even wondered about openness, or whether the person he hired shut people up. Or shut them off, preventing them from being themselves.

He's the guy who wants to keep us on the treadmill of refraining, rather than encouraging us, urging us onto the highroad of risk and discovery and being. Instead of growing in recognition and obedience to an inner knowing, he lives under the law—standards outside himself. He loves the dead thing—the law, the state, the party, the organization. He sees people as things to keep the Sabbath, things to carry out the policies and plans of the Church or other institutions.

St. Paul sent out a warning concerning Mr. Snodgrass, in case you aren't aware of it: "If then you have died with Christ to material ways of looking at things and have escaped the world's crude and elemental notions and teachings of externalism, why do you live as if you still belong to the world? Why do you submit to rules and regulations such as:

>   Do not handle this,
>   Do not taste that,
>   Do not even touch them,

referring to things all of which perish with being used. To do this is to follow human precepts and doctrines."

Mr. Snodgrass isn't going to let you in on the truth that Jesus wasn't as concerned with the law as he was with his work of changing people. He's a guy that subconsciously knows that the only thing that matters is something he hasn't got—love. Underneath he knows that morality is the by-product of love, and what appears as morality may be simply an absence of passion.

Ellie lives in a nearby apartment building, and this morning she is incensed because she finds in her mailbox five pages, single-spaced, of instructions concerning rules for living in their apartment. She tells me the reason for the new rules. Older people take their dogs to the sandboxes small children play in and actually let their dogs use the sandboxes, fully realizing the danger.

"No wonder they have to have rules," she says. "They have no love. No sensitivity. They have to have someone outside themselves threaten them and tell them what is right and wrong, just like small children. Laws are necessary not because people don't know better—only because people don't love."

You can spot the legalist by his definitions (even though those definitions aren't very often verbal). Good, to Mr. Snodgrass, is an absence. An absence of argument. An absence of resistance. An absence of struggle. Truth could be defined as "an absence of lies." This is why he seldom talks to his wife. If he doesn't tell her a lie, he believes he has told her the truth.

Being good? What is being good? Being good is simply not being bad. Not doing bad things. Bad things are actions outside oneself. Lack of response isn't bad to Mr. Snodgrass. Neither is lack of caring. Neither is selfishness. Or a mind two inches wide. Or wanting to be the center of the universe, around whom everyone else revolves.

What would it mean to be "loved" by Mr. Snodgrass? Well, loving you means not saying bad things about you. Not kicking you down the stairs. Wiping his feet on the welcome home mat as he comes home from work. He pleases you by not tying you to the foot of the bed and starving you. By not being late to dinner. He likes you best when you are gone on a trip to your mother's.

One observation: Don't do unto Mr. Snodgrass as he does to others. He wouldn't like his wife to apply his immature concept of good to the food she cooks for him. Wouldn't like it if her main concern would be not to put poison in his food. Or if she didn't care that it had positive "goodness"—that it was nutritious, that it looks good ("I believe I'll put green food coloring in his scrambled eggs this morning"), that it tastes good, that it provides emotional satisfaction ("Here, Mr. S., you can eat this in the back bedroom alone. I'll eat in the kitchen").

This may be a little hard to explain, but isn't it true that when you are wrapped up in rules, fighting something negative like "not going to church" or even standing for something negative like "not going to movies," that it turns out that what you are fighting isn't even a "thing." It doesn't exist. (This is why evil is more than an absence of good.) An absence of something has no existence except as an appearance. Stupidity is a good example. Stupidity is an absence. Stupidity is not a thing in itself. It turns up in stupid behavior and appears as a thing, but is actually only an absence. An absence of intelligence. An appearance with no root in reality.

"Whatsoever *things* you desire when you pray," Jesus promised, "believe that you receive them and you will have them." What did he mean by *things*? What did St. Paul mean in the Love Chapter when he wrote that the lover "believeth all things, endureth all things, hopeth all things"? Did he mean I'm to believe any Harv that comes along? That I'm to endure my child kicking me in the shins when he wants a new Mercedes and I don't give it to him? That I'm to hope that I'll make straight A's when I haven't cracked a book since September?

I have to know what a thing is. A thing is an action or product consistent with its nature or process. A thing is neither the process without the product, nor is it the product without the process. A thing is a whole. When I'm told that if I forgive others I'll be forgiven, that's a whole thing. Forgiveness is the fruit or product — but forgiveness goes with my forgiving others.

Esau is a good example of a man who didn't want a "thing," but who begged God for a fantasy. He wanted the blessing, prayed for it earnestly and with tears after he had given it away. But God couldn't give it to him, not because God was in a bad mood or peevish. God couldn't give it to him because God doesn't deal in absurdities, but in substance. The blessing was only part of a whole thing, and it happened to be the reward of the responsibilities inherent in the birthright. Esau was said to have despised the birthright and because the blessing was simply the reward of the birthright he despised, God couldn't give it to him.

The person who deals in fantasies and absurdities will think he wants a happy marriage, even though he insists on living like Bachelor Button, even though he lives a closed-off, isolated existence, refusing to give the time of day to his family. He will want to be believed even though he has seldom been known to tell the truth, except by accident. He wants to be considered a Christian even though he despises process and perception and considers forgiveness as "chickening out," or true humility as "stupidity."

Donny is a boy who thinks good is the reward he should get for not being bad, not taking drugs, and not fooling around with women. He doesn't understand why he doesn't get good grades in school even though he prays for good grades. After all, he wasn't on drugs, he tells God. Didn't have women, he tells God. Always tried not to be bad, he tells God.

I hope some adult points out to him, gently, that there is no known connection between not having women and good grades. That there *is* some relationship between studying and good grades. The prayer Donny would see answered would be the prayer for a whole thing—that God will help him to study and to understand, and then grades will be simply the reward of that understanding.

Trying to please anyone, even God, by *not* doing certain things is ridiculous. You never please, as the legalist believes, by *not* displeasing.

Of course there are dozens of things I would do if I didn't want to displease. I wouldn't forget to brush my teeth. I wouldn't forget to take a bath. But you can't call *not* doing certain things actually pleasing someone. All I would be doing is *not* disgusting people, *not* turning them off. Pleasing is a positive thing.

And the reason you can't read how to please anyone in a book is because pleasing is really a very sensitive, creative, and highly individualistic thing that depends upon your knowledge of the other person's values.

A guy who puts a big premium on the money he's stashed away at First Federal isn't going to be ecstatic at his wife standing at his front door, idly awaiting his return in a gorgeous negligee. In the first place, the negligee cost money, didn't it? In the second place, why isn't she out working? She could be earning another deposit at First!

But the insensitive person will go on buying her husband gifts when he despises gifts, and then feel slighted when he gets angry, "because I am showing my love in the only way I know how."

Trying to please another person by not doing certain things without finding out what he values is like trying to please God by keeping the law. It isn't possible. All you will do is not disgust God. Without faith it is impossible to please God—and faith is more than not doing certain things. It's the gorgeous, open attitude, a meek and realistic and quiet spirit which is of great value in the sight of God. Just as I would be sick-to-my-stomach with a twenty-year-old son who is still obeying and keeping rules and yet is still unable to catch my meaning, get my humor, glimpse my vision, so I feel that God is pleased with me when I have this receptive faith that is waiting eagerly to catch God's meaning, get his humor, and glimpse his vision.

SEVEN
THE PRETENDER

If I had to name the one big problem facing young people today in their homes, schools, and churches, without a doubt it would be hypocrisy. It was the one sin intolerable even to Jesus, so I can only imagine the frustration of a child raised by hypocritical parents. This child vaguely feels that there is "something terribly wrong," but generally assumes that thing to be his own perception because he doesn't have the ability yet to understand and analyze what is going on.

Oldy Brown used to be my idea of a hypocrite. He would cheat his own mother out of fifteen cents if he had a chance—and then come to church on Sunday morning, take up the offering (I always figured he pocketed at least 10 percent of the proceeds), and think he was doing a fantastic snow job on everyone in the community.

Now I see that Oldy was the more harmless kind of hypocrite. I doubt that he ever fooled himself for a minute. He went to church because his wife wanted to present a picture of a religious family to the town. He wasn't going to let her down. He performed for Hannah on Sunday and did his own number on the rest of the town the rest of the week. Oldy probably loved Sunday. Sunday gave him time out to get it all together. It was a chance to sit in church, look over the audience, and line up all the old ladies he was going to fleece come Monday morning.

Now there's a different form of hypocrisy. My friend is a classic example. Jennifer says she has a problem. Jennifer says she doesn't know whether people like her for *her* or for her good looks.

"You obviously like that kind of attention," I say.

Of course she denies that. "I'd do anything to get rid of this curse; it's as if I wore a sign across my chest."

"I really don't believe what you say. I notice that you sort of *encourage* attention."

"What do I do to encourage it?"

"Well, I'd rather not go into it—but okay, the way you dress."

"You don't understand; this is the way the girls dress on campus," she pouts.

"That's right. Girls. Girls that want attention. You happen to be a thirty-year-old mother who claims not to want that attention."

"I suppose you don't think I look good in shorts," she whimpers, crossing her long, slim, well-tanned legs.

"Who *cares*? You are the one who says she has a problem she wants to get rid of. I was just offering a suggestion. You seem to me like the guy who spends his life slaving for a million dollars, gets it, then says he wishes he wasn't rich."

"Listen," she says, growing sober and looking profound. (Now I want you to listen to what this woman says, very closely, or you won't believe it.) "I feel it is psychologically good for me to wear shorts. It keeps me humble because I have these ugly stretch marks."

I couldn't believe it. I simply couldn't *believe* it. You could imagine a guy as old as Oldy being able to think up some devious thing like that—but a woman thirty years old? "Hey,"

I say, seeing what I am up against, "I've got to go pick up the film at the drug store."

I think of hypocrisy as a split between what I am (my heart) and what I think I am (my head). You see, I used to have the idea that the hypocrite purposely acted in one way and preached or professed the opposite. That is true at the beginning—at one time we *do* see clearly. But we all, like sheep, have gone astray; there is a point of departure. And Jennifer is now a real pro. And real pros are unaware—they are blind to their own emptiness, lack of love, hostility, arrogance, manipulation, secretiveness, and defensiveness.

"Father, forgive them, for they know not what they do," was not an excuse or a rationalization, but a description of blindness, whether that blindness was national or personal.

I wonder if the book of James isn't actually about hypocrisy. Not just a book showing the conflict between faith and works, but also between *words* and works. James says that your faith (what you really believe) shows itself in what you do, not what you say. For example, if a woman refuses to tell her husband anything that goes on in her head or in her life, if she hides everything, she is actually saying that she believes what she does is none of his business, even though she may teach a class on the importance of marital communication and openness between husband and wife.

James shows how the hypocrite reacts to a problem of cold and hunger. Does he tell the cold, hungry guy to go get lost? Does he kick him out the door so the guy will feel justified in despising him? No, he's more clever than that—or more blind to his own intentions. He doesn't want to help the man, but he wants to keep up appearances. He doesn't want the man to dislike him, so in place of food and clothes, he offers words. "Be thou warmed and fed," he says sweetly to the cold, hungry man standing at his door, and the man goes away colder and hungrier than he was when he came to the door, but thinking (if he's like I was for years), "What a nice guy lives there."

Applied to marriage, it would be like a wife being too sick to get the work done. Vacuuming needs to be done. Piles of dirty dishes are stacked in the sink with spaghetti sauce hardened from last night — and her husband says as he starts out the door, "If there's anything I can do to help you around here, please let me know. I'm so sorry you are sick. Have a good day."

No matter how kindly he says those words, if he doesn't care enough to run the water, add the soap, and do the dishes, but only pretends with glowing words that he deeply cares, that's hypocrisy. Using words as a substitute for caring is hypocrisy. Real caring, as James says, always leads to appropriate action.

The truth is that intentions are revealed by behavior. My faith is shown by my works. If I constantly speak in an irritable tone of voice and yet claim not to have any "bad" feelings or intentions, I am turning off the message of my own words. If my child asks me, "How come you are more friendly to that hateful rich man than you are to nice Mrs. Frump?" and I shame my child for saying such a thing, and I fail to look at my behavior, then I am turning off the message of my own actions.

Or if I'd say, "I'll try harder to be more friendly to Mrs. Frump next time," (thinking that my child has only seen a behavior rather than a motivation), that's equally as dangerous. I'm afraid of reaching the place where I am unable to stop, evaluate, and think to myself, "Hey there, I better check up on my values. When I begin to cater to the rich and ignore the poor, there's something wrong."

This must have happened in the early Church. Communion was a time to come together for self-examination before

God and because there were those who came to the table unworthily, " . . . for this cause there are many sick among you —and many sleep."

Wilbur is one of my principals—a guy concerned primarily with appearances. Wilbur is concerned that his marriage look like a good marriage and cares nothing about the relationship itself. If his wife had a drinking problem, Wilbur wouldn't deal with the problem or try to get help for her. He would simply do anything he could to keep the neighbors or anyone else from knowing.

He's the guy intent on appearing intelligent. He is not at all problem-centered. It normally takes years of growth to see through appearances, and therefore we are usually very slow to see through people like Wilbur, to realize that they are more concerned with appearing concerned than with the concern itself. Sometimes the truth of that hits us all of a sudden.

I was trying to discuss a problem with Wilbur. There I was, thrashing the problem around, trying to understand the problem better myself, and at the same time trying to get Wilbur's insight on the problem. Suddenly it dawned on me that I was talking to a person who wasn't concerned with understanding this or any other problem at all. Understanding had no value to him whatsoever. I suddenly felt very alone, and I knew there would be no help from his direction.

And I felt weary. I realized I might as well dig up a cadaver and talk to it for all the help I would get.

There Wilbur sat, his head in his hands, careful not to mess his hair up. Wilbur wears his hair—well, you would have to see it to believe the creativity involved in the style. Apparently he is balding. In order to hide his problem, Wilbur has had his hairdresser create a new problem for him. He took all the hair in back, grew it long, flopped it over the front, then cut it in Mamie Eisenhower bangs. It's really different. You might like it a lot.

Wilbur has deep furrows in his forehead—permanent furrows from worrying over big things like making milk money balance. I guess you're aware by now that the first sign of neurosis is that the person concerned has very loused-up values. I mean by this that what is important to the normal person has little or no importance to the neurotic. What seems trivial and unimportant to the normal person carries great weight with the neurotic.

Wilbur has made a practice of hiring teachers with a genius for destroying students with humiliation. These are teachers concerned with form, who care nothing about content. One student, for example, spent three weeks on a report on Winston Churchill. I never saw a kid so excited about a character as that kid was about Churchill. The boy had a bad memory, turned the report in a day late, and the teacher gave him a zero. She obviously cared nothing about the boy's interest. She was a person whose main goal was to be respected and obeyed.

When I told Wilbur I was concerned about these teachers, Wilbur agreed that he, too, was concerned about them. I sighed with relief, thinking we could get right down to discussing the problem.

Just at that point I remembered that I had read the evaluations Wilbur himself had written on two of these teachers last year. Wilbur had rated both of them as excellent, top-rate teachers. So rather than tell Wilbur my specific worries about the two teachers, I asked Wilbur why he now felt this "concern" about them.

"Several times they arrived with their students at least three minutes late at the lunch line—and you know we just don't have any time to spare."

I am staring at the space above and to the right of Wilbur's right ear.

"And on top of that," Wilbur complains, "their students

have been boisterous at least twice while waiting in the hall. You know we can't put up with that. It looks bad!"

"I know, Wilbur," my voice echoes weakly from a spot only slightly above the top of my desk, suddenly aware that Wilbur's idea of a good teacher is a person who keeps up appearances.

I told Wilbur of the many complaints, legitimate complaints, concerning these teachers. Asked him if he had any idea what went on in his teachers' classrooms. Wilbur takes this personally. Droops his head and pouts, as he always does whenever his views are challenged. He is hoping he can make me sorry I ever questioned his Noble Concerns.

Wilbur's furrows deepen and with a slight tremble in his voice he tells me how much he loves children. How he loves to sit down on the floor in the middle of the room and discuss things of concern with them. How he loves to watch them learn and be part of the learning process. Why, to hear Wilbur talk there is nothing he likes better than to spend his time with his students. A solid gold Cadillac couldn't please Wilbur as much as spending his time with the beloved students. He nearly had me reaching for my handkerchief.

I recovered my poise enough to ask Wilbur how long it had been since he had spent an hour in any classroom in the building. How long it had been since he sat down to observe or be a part of the learning process.

Wilbur hesitated, took off his glasses, and chewed on the stems of them in his effort to appear grave and ponderous. He—well, actually he couldn't remember the last time.

As usual, Wilbur was all words. He hadn't visited a classroom all year. He didn't care. This time I realized what I had been feeling about him. I couldn't put it into words. You hear him talk and it feels like the thin coating of ice that covers a pond with the first freeze—it can't take pressure or it will crack (Wilbur even likes to admit he can't take stress!). You feel that what he says is superficial, hasn't been grappled with or struggled with, and hasn't been really seen. It is not real—not connected and rooted to any deep thinking and caring. Because there is no real inner involvement, the performers, like Wilbur, often come off looking terrifically "nice." There is no gnashing of teeth, no deep involvement that shows itself in hair pulling, anger, joy, and other things that would be unattractive to Wilbur.

"How careful you Pharisees are about the outside, but how negligent you are about the inside," Jesus said of the hypocrites, the one and only class of people he couldn't abide. And then he gave the reason for hypocrisy: "You are they that justify yourselves before man but God knoweth your heart, for that which is highly esteemed among men is an abomination in the sight of God." The cause of hypocrisy is wrong values—esteeming the outside of things, caring nothing for what really matters.

The growing person moves away from phoniness to realness. Nathaniel Branden defines realness: "To be real, in a psychological sense, means to be . . . integrated in thought, feeling, and bodily behavior. For example, when a person professes to be cheerful and carefree but we see that his movements are abrupt and jerky and his voice and speech betray a current of irritability we do not necessarily conclude that he is consciously lying, but we say that he is cut off from his emotions, he is not integrated. . . . To cease to know what one feels is to cease to experience what things mean to one—which is to be cut off from one's own context."

To grow toward realness, I become aware that "as a man thinks in his *heart*," as he understands, perceives, knows, sees, that this is the real self, and the conscious self either reflects this self accurately, lets it be, lets it shine, or denies this inner self. This suppression of truth is a process as outlined in Romans 1; the truly phony person can come to the place that he is absolutely convinced that he is sending no unconscious messages. He is enraged if someone sees that equality is only a fancy theory to him—that while he speaks glowingly of racial equality, he despises fat people, or would choose a beautiful girl as his secretary in preference to someone qualified.

Now I begin to notice conflicts between what I say and how I really think. Between my head (my theories) and my heart (how I really see things). I find some pretty wide chasms. I'm like a dorm mother I knew when I was in school. She often lectured about materialism. What a curse materialism is. One evening she starts to cry when she is speaking at a dorm meeting. Crying about the plight of the Eastern countries. Because they weren't free? She didn't mention that. Because they couldn't worship God openly? No, no mention of that. What had deeply distressed her was the fact that the free world had a monopoly on material possessions—it owned 85 percent of the world's refrigerators. (This concern from the same lady with the sermons on materialism.) You sort of wanted to go up to her and say—well, it's as if she had a dirty slip hanging three inches below a beautiful dress—you'd want to say something. Tell her something. Maybe I could have said, "Pardon me, dearie— your values are showing."

EIGHT
THE POSSESSOR

If you'd like an unsolicited insight, one connection I've seen lately is that the growth (or lack of it) of the people I know is directly related to whether their own personal values are growing and changing. If they cling to anything, whether a person or a dog or the house they live in, then pfffft—no growth.

Meg doesn't really cling to possessions, but has focused her time and attention on her beauty and sex appeal. Meg tells me there is no one she couldn't have married if she had wanted to. A former President almost killed himself over her and once a guy by the name of Bob something-or-other went to an insane asylum when she said no.

And there's Robert who prides himself on what he refers to as his "counseling ability." He considers it his spiritual gift. Everyone else considers it a definite curse. His sister is delirious with grief over her husband who has just left her and Robert delivers her his Baggy Pantyhose lecture. He says he shouldn't have done it, but that it's hard to love a woman with baggy pantyhose, especially when she's twenty pounds overweight. Besides, he remembers that she complained at Husband when she caught him filching money from her purse (money she had finally borrowed from her father to pay the light bill ten days overdue). Robert tells you he was the one to advise Kennedy to get into politics. He also warned Kennedy not to go to Dallas.

There's Fredda, who thinks family is all important. She can't like anyone, she says, who doesn't have a happy marriage. "Gee, Fredda," I say, "that sounds unfair. Sounds like my friend Jenny who wouldn't speak to her neighbor with thyroid trouble because her mother had warned her never to trust a person with bug eyes."

"I don't care," Fredda argues. "Anyone who can't get along in a marriage has to have something wrong with him."

"Look, Fredda," I say, "I honestly wish you'd married a psychopath. It would have been good for your compassion."

Then there's this guy who thinks his honor is the most important thing, the thing he must protect at all cost. He tells me he cannot forgive a friend and explains the reason: "If a person insults my—what do you call it—*ehr*, I do not speak to that person again."

What does he mean? His name? His status? I look up the word in my German dictionary while he waits. "*Ehr.* Oh, honor? You don't speak to a person again if he insults your honor?"

"No," he states flatly. "I will not speak to him again. I will not see him again. If he is in the same room I do not see him again. Not tomorrow. Not in five days. Not in five months. Not in five years."

"Well," I comment, "what a big scary person you are—it's just whooosh like that, huh?" What I wanted to say was, "No wonder you've been married four times and are looking for a job again."

Then he proceeds to tell about his numerous jobs. "If someone, my boss, wants me to do something, he must say please, and if he says please, he must *mean* please."

"You do not forgive?" I ask. He doesn't understand. Back to my trusty little dictionary. *"Verzeihen?"* I ask.

"Ah no, no," he says as the light dawns. "I do not. I cannot. It is not in my heart to — what you say — forgive."

Then there's Harold. Harold is a getter. Not like Scrooge, the typical tightwad. Or Silas Marner. Harold is the guy across the street who has developed arthritis of the neck from watching out his window with frog-green envy to see if anyone across the street or down the block has anything new. Harold isn't interested only in having. He's also interested in *having had*, past tense. "I don't know if I'll ever get this stuff paid for, but one thing for sure, even if I have to trade it in, I can at least say when a guy shows me his boat — yeah, I've had one too. If he has a new motorcycle, I can say — sure, I've had one of those too."

Erich Fromm's thesis in *To Have or To Be* is that if you don't have the right priorities you are in for trouble as an individual, and we are in for trouble as a society. "A new society can be brought about only if a profound change occurs in the human heart — if a new object of devotion takes the place of the present one."

"Having" as an orientation has to do with more than material possessions, of course. There's the neighbor boy who thinks loving means having. Owning. Possessing. He doesn't want to know what his girl friend is reading. He wants to know where the heck she's *been* the last two hours. He doesn't want to know what she's thinking about. He wants to know why the heck she didn't phone him when he told her to.

You can also *have* experiences. I've actually known "Christian" people group together according to the *experiences* they've had rather than the person who is at the center of these experiences.

The Bible speaks of *having* knowledge, as in the sentence:

"Though I have all knowledge and have not love, I am nothing. . . ." "Having" knowledge is a past experience—a dead thing—but present response is a living interaction with reality.

Today I see what "having all knowledge" might mean. This is Christus Himmelfahrt. Ascension Day. Commemorating the day Christ went back to heaven. And many of the Germans observe this by taking walks together. I went on a six-hour walk with a group and we stopped at various cafes along the way to rest. In Cafe De'ml there is a mother playing with her baby. I am thinking how the mother enjoys her baby. You can see it all over her face. Just then one of the men in the group points to the mother and says, "Look there. That is a bad mother."

"Why do you say that?" I ask, already suspecting the answer.

"Look, the baby's arms are not covered. The baby is cold."

I don't feel like much more of this rigid thinking today. "Yeah," I say, "the baby does look a trifle cold."

This guy isn't finished. "No good mother would allow her baby to be cold."

"Wow, I don't know. That baby might get a little cold physically—but she's certainly going to get plenty of emotional warmth from her mother."

The discussion didn't last much longer on that subject, but as we got up to leave and started off again on our hike, I jumped a puddle, didn't quite make it, got one shoe a little wet.

"Wipe it off," this same man orders, taking his handkerchief out of his pocket. "You will get a cold."

"What is *wrong* with this guy?" I ask myself. "Ahhhh," I exclaim, "colds are caused by wet feet!"

He looks at me as if I'm from outer space. "Anyone knows that," he says.

"Maybe. Maybe not. All I know is that I've never gotten a cold from wet feet," I mumble.

This kind of thing has gone on all day, and I'm weary of it. Weary of rigidity. Weary of old patterns of thinking based on worn-out premises. Weary of people who never wonder. Only this morning a couple tells me of some of the cruel punishments they have inflicted on their child because of his messiness, and I am appalled.

"You think not keeping his bicycle shiny is wrong? Bad?" I ask. "You think messiness is *wicked*?"

They both look at me, then at each other, then as if they are going to break into a run. I suddenly feel like John the Baptist, crying in the wilderness. No one has apparently ever questioned the values of these people.

"Why, anyone knows not taking good care of things is wrong. Anyone knows messiness is wrong," the lady says. "Anyone knows."

We change the subject to corn pads and how effective they are for blisters. And not only for blisters, but for callouses and corns — my, *my*.

And suddenly, several hours after the walk, I see something. I see why Christ said we had to die before we could live. That these old rigid patterns have to be broken before one can think and see freshly; and they cannot be broken as long as my pride remains intact. As long as this conviction inside me persists that I am in-the-know, as long as I'm leaning on my own understanding, as long as my trust in my own answers remains unbroken, nothing new or fresh will have a chance to surface, giving me the energy to grow.

Love grows away from preoccupation with having knowledge (which is not the same as intelligence). Theodore Reik in *Listening With the Third Ear* writes: "The overvaluation of intelligence among cultured people in our country has reached a frightening degree. Not only our public schools and our colleges and universities but also our research institutes give the impression that the intelligence test is the only criterion of man's mental endowment. It is as if other gifts were not even to be considered, as if imagination, moral courage, creative faculties were of no importance."

One teen-ager was telling of the dilemma in his home: "My parents think the whole purpose of communication is winning. Or at least appearing to win by being the one in-the-know. My dad thinks if I try to discuss anything with him I'm trying to persuade him rather than understand something better. He has a whole repertoire of stories where it was him against the world—and *he* turned out right."

Another thing many people take pride in "having" is a happy marriage. Ronda was telling me that her marriage had to fall apart before she saw she was putting it first. It was her priest who helped point her problem out to her—that the first commandment is, Love the Lord God with all your heart, soul, and mind. That the biggest favor one person can do for another is to see meaning in his own life, so he doesn't have to depend on the other person for his whole reason for existence. The weight is too heavy. . . .

"And me—you know what it did for me, putting this first?" Ronda asks. "When you put anything first before loving and living out God's will, you start getting really fearful and insecure, even a little nutty. Sort of paranoid really. If you put survival first, then you're going to experience all kinds of yukky, sicky fears every time the least thing threatens your life."

It wasn't long before Ronda found that her "new discovery" wouldn't be popular among "Christian" groups. She was telling me about a Protestant women's group she attended soon after her big discovery. The course was to have been a Bible study, but disintegrated into a lecture on how to be fascinating and keep your husband happy.

Ronda listened carefully and politely through the lesson.

"You know, it seems to me that centering on my own sexual happiness and the sexual happiness of my husband, on my own security and well-being—well, I see it as idolatry," Ronda finally suggests.

The room grew silent.

Ronda is Catholic, not used to Protestant women's groups, and she began to stammer, uncomfortable with what she interpreted as cold silence. "Well, gee, I mean it seems there's a danger in jumping over the first commandment to the commandment having to do with loving others. . . ."

Total silence. Finally the teacher cleared her throat. "You see, Ronda," Teacher said in a corrective voice, "having a happy marriage *is* God's will. You see, it's like this, Ronda—you put God first by putting your husband first."

Ronda is a fairly new Christian who had spent the last year not doing an awful lot except digging into the Bible. "Wow, I don't like to contradict you, I'm so new at all this, but it seems to me that an idea like yours is going to lead you into a conflict. It seems to me that Jesus implied that it's entirely possible that the Christian's new allegiance, new responses, new priorities, new understanding and attitudes may result in the problem that his worst enemies may be those of his own household."

"I think we are getting away from our lesson," Teacher gurgled cheerfully, wanting to regain control. "Now ladies, let's continue with our discussion of the kind of clothes men like their gals to wear. . . ."

Nothing is worth having at the expense of truth. Nathaniel Branden wrote: "It should be recognized that the desire to have a harmonious and benevolent relationship . . . is a rational one; it is not, *per se*, a breach of proper independence. It becomes a breach only if and when a man subordinates his mind and judgment to that desire above his perception of reality. If and when the price of harmony with his fellowmen becomes the surrender of his mind, a psychologically healthy man does not pay it; nothing can be a benefit to him at that cost."

NINE
THE PLEASER

Carl Rogers, in defining the value-directions of the growing person, says, "They tend to move away from meeting the expectations of others. Pleasing others as a goal in itself is negatively valued."

People-pleasing is another form of hanging-on that prevents growth. Paul went so far as to say, "Do I seek to please men? If I seek to please men, I should not be the servant of Christ." And this isn't some rule someone thought up in the middle of the night. It is actually true that society has always opposed individual thinking, individual development, individual understanding and interpretation. This is especially true of that society called the Church.

The way away from people-pleasing was a long process for me. I was the type of person who would answer an absurd request for "sixteen dozen chocolate chip cookies by tomorrow morning" with "Sure, I'd love to. Sixteen dozen? Sure. Sure, I understand the other mothers work. Sure, kid, as I say, I understand. What day did you say? Tomorrow? By 9:00 tomorrow morning? Well, yeah it is. I say *yeah*, it *is* a little late to get them baked, but sure."

Alice was one of the friends I had during what I think of

now as my pre-awareness stage. It was fall, a beautiful September, and school had just begun. The summer had been long and hot, but on this cool morning I had perked a pot of coffee, just for myself, before the children left for school. Then I followed the children to the door and locked it carefully behind them.

I checked the back door. Yep, it was locked. I poured a steaming cup of good black coffee and sank down into the deep pillows of a favorite chair in the living room.

"This is *great*. Absolutely great. This is what you call luxury. A quiet house. A morning alone. . . ."

Just then someone knocked at the door. "Good grief," I thought. "Oh, help. Just help. It's Alice. Gotta be Alice at the door again. Probably wants to help. Probably wants to paint the house this morning or something like that. No, she wants to dig up bulbs. I can't stand another morning of this. Tell you what, old girl, don't answer that door. Hear? Alice is why you locked it anyway."

The knocking stopped. The doorbell started to ring. It rang and rang and rang. How could I face another day of Alice? Another *hour* of Alice? Alice who insisted on helping me do my work, roll my hair, hoe my garden, give advice on childrearing—while her own house looked like the Original Disaster Area, and her children, I imagined, already belonged to the Mafia.

Alice was the let's-do-it-again type who is always looking for a friend to make a Habit of. If I invited her to go with me to my favorite cafe on Monday, she wouldn't say, "Thanks a lot, that was fun." She would say, "Let's do this every Monday." The all-or-nothing type who either watches your front door constantly so you can't sneak to the store without her, or else totally ignores you.

"Maybe it's not Alice," I thought momentarily. The ringing continued and I made a lunge for the door. "Oh, sit back down. Of course it's Alice. Sure, it's Alice. Got to be Alice. Who else comes unannounced and uninvited at 8:00 in the morning? No one, that's who. No one."

So I set my jaw and decided to continue enjoying the coffee I'd thought was so good only a few moments before. "Going to enjoy this coffee if it kills me. Going to enjoy this coffee if I choke on it."

As suddenly as the racket had begun, the knocking and bell ringing stopped. "See how easy it is," I began to congratulate myself. "Just don't answer the door. She'll go away."

I close my eyes. Sink down, down, down further into the chair, my hands fold over my chest like a mummy, when suddenly I hear the unmistakable sound of shattering glass.

I fly through the house, dash down the basement steps. There, in one of the basement windows, hangs one skinny, hairy leg, dangling through a broken window. "Oh, *there* you are," Alice was shouting hoarsely through the window. "Boy, am I relieved. I was afraid you were sick or hurt or something."

Now how can you be mean to someone like that? How can you tell her to drop out of your life pronto, if not before? Thoreau said once that if a man came to his house with the conscious purpose of doing him good, he would run for his life. Well, not me. I felt guilty, really guilty. Felt guilty for needing time to think. Time to be alone. So I invited Alice back upstairs, gave her some Band-Aids (I didn't feel guilty enough to actually apply them), poured her a cup of coffee, and apologized for not answering the door.

One of the main things I remember about Alice is that she is one of the first people on whom I tried Norman Vincent Peale's *Power of Positive Thinking*. I thought it would make a great experiment. When Alice would come—that's her over there, slurping her third cup of coffee—I would direct positive thinking vibes toward her. (I called them prayer waves, if you can believe that.) Silently, of course. "Go. Go. Go *home*.

H-o-m-e, Alice. Your kids are calling you, Alice. *Go.*" And then I'd turn to God: "Help Alice to go home, God. She isn't doing anything grotesque or disgusting unless you consider slurping as disgusting as I do, but I just want her to leave. Make her leave, God. If you don't make her leave, I'll . . . I'll . . . I don't know what I'll do. Please?"

But of course Alice wouldn't budge. Maybe I need to explain right here that Alice wasn't simply an isolated instance of my way of thinking at that time — it was clearly a manifestation of a whole dominating principle that ruled my life. I yielded my life passively and constantly to be shaped and formed by the schedule (or lack of schedule) of people around me. After all, it was selfish to care about what I wanted, wasn't it? After all, I'm supposed to love people, aren't I?

It's now five years later. Five years after that Alice incident. A friend calls up. "Hey kid," she begins, "can you keep Shirl for me? She has diarrhea and I really hate to take her with me to Mom's today. I mean, Mom might get it."

"Hey, really sorry, Mare," I chirp, not a drop of guilt in my voice for anyone to latch onto. "I'm on my way to the library and just can't do it."

What happened during those years? I learned the divine order of life, and I learned what "loving your neighbor" means — at least a little of what it means.

Love is a trinity, and the person who wants wisdom begins to see the divine order of life: first, to respond (to value, prefer, search for the principle or meaning of the messages and experiences of life, to actually hunger, thirst, mourn for wisdom); second, to perceive (to understand, see what you were seeking); third, freedom to act (allowing this inner work and new understanding to find its own expression without ordering it or commanding it). In the first place, you *can't* command the inner work and process of the Spirit; in the second place, this work of the Spirit is more like bearing a child or raising wheat than it is like baking a cake. *You* don't tell the crops when to ripen, the crops tell you what to do. You don't tell the life within you what to do or when to finish the process — this inner life dictates to you.

I've noticed that all messed-up-ness comes from disregarding this order. Maybe you can observe the process and order (respond, understand, act) from what happened to me during those five years I told you about.

One Sunday morning shortly after the Alice incident I went to church. The minister preached a sermon on loving your neighbor as yourself. So while the people around me jumped up and began to plan togetherness picnics and knee-deep-in-love conferences, I went into a slump. I remembered my old Ma's advice that truth would reveal itself to me if I really wanted it, so I told God I hadn't the slightest idea what he meant by loving my neighbor as myself. I told him I'd wait right there until he let me in on the meaning. Somehow I knew that the way out of people-pleasing wasn't forcing myself out but, as always, *seeing* my way out.

"Maybe love is a warm feeling toward people," I thought. So I tried very hard to have nice warm feelings toward people. If someone poked me in the ribs with an umbrella when I was uptown shopping (the people in the country I lived in at that time used umbrellas as weapons), I would smile a slightly curdly smile and try to work up a nice warm feeling for that person. Once I even managed to say a prayer for a man who gave me such a jab in the stomach with his umbrella I knew for sure I would die of internal bleeding. (Bless that cute little man, God. He's kinda cute, isn't he? Those full, fat little cheeks that look like a squirrel storing nuts for the winter.)

I don't remember the exact incident that did in that definition of love. Maybe it was the morning my neighbor's dog,

Fred, left a deposit outside the door of our apartment that my husband slipped on. Whatever, I could never love if a nice warm feeling was God's idea of love.

Maybe loving my neighbor means knowing my neighbor, I thought. "Maybe you have to know about people to care for them," I said, more to myself than anyone else. So I would ask the milkman about his wife, inquire about his children, try at least to remember his name, even if I couldn't remember Albrecht, Adolph, Hans, or Georg.

And just about the time my poor memory would get it down pat, I would get a new milkman. And besides, my baloney detector wouldn't let me by with this definition of love. "Knowing isn't caring," I grumble. "If love isn't an emotion, isn't an activity of the will, isn't knowledge, then how about you helping me, God? You promised, remember? You promised to give wisdom, to show meaning to anyone who asks."

Days went by. Was God, after all, like some rigid mother who sets her baby into some awful timetable which is alien and conflicting with her baby's needs? Then why didn't God show me? Right now? "How do I love my neighbor as myself?"

One day I am absently listening to a friend praise a teacher she looks up to. To hear her monologue, no one in the world exists like the person she is praising. He's so handsome. So smart. Went to the best theology school in the nation. So talented. Gee, is he smart. She looks up to him. Worships at his feet. If he would tell her to head for the hills because Jesus was up there waiting, she would go.

I get a very gentle and familiar nudge.

"Huh?" I ask, alert now. "There's nothing wrong with admiration. *Is* there, God?"

"Here's a picture for you to look at," the thought comes.

"Whudga mean?" I ask.

"Remember your question?"

"I remember."

"Your friend doesn't love her neighbor as herself."
"She doesn't?"
"She doesn't."
"Ah, hah," I laugh aloud, "loving my neighbor as myself has nothing to do with doing (although it will reveal itself in what I do). Loving my neighbor as myself has to do with my values. It is neither looking up to my neighbor, putting him on a pedestal. Or looking down on him. It's a way of seeing my neighbor that results from right values—seeing him as my equal." That's why equality can't be legislated—because equality is a way of seeing. A way of seeing people a little as God sees them—not according to outer trappings and appearances. Not bowing to talent or charm or personality as I did when I put the things first that are an abomination in the sight of God.

Now, you don't love your neighbor as yourself by trying to love your neighbor as yourself. Only when you give God your devotion—only then can you possibly love your neighbor as a person, rather than as the talented woman, or the rich man, or the brilliant child. To begin to love means you must begin to look to what you put first.

"So that's it?" I cackle, pretty happy with this revealer inside of me somewhere. "That's what old James was saying all along. That's what he meant when he said we are breaking this law of our Lord's (to love our neighbor as ourselves) when we favor the rich and fawn over them."

To love my neighbor as myself? I begin to see it means a lot of other things. It means I have to be in touch with my own feelings, reactions, likes, and dislikes before I know how to treat you. If I don't like the feeling of being used, then if I love you as myself, I will not use you. I won't expect more of you than I am willing to give. If I don't want to loan you money (I don't), I won't expect you to loan me money. If I chafe when you impose your will on me (even if you temporarily manipulate me into thinking it's my idea), then I won't do that to you. If selfishness makes me seethe, if loud talking embarrasses me ("Please, Bertha, can't you see the people at that table are staring at us? Don't talk out loud in the library, Bertha—especially about your hysterectomy! Shhhh, Bertha, please shush"), if putrid odors revolt me, then if I love you as myself, I will act accordingly.

This is then my secret of loving others as myself—to be so in touch with myself that I don't have to have the law outside of me telling me what to do. I see that you are tired, that it is midnight, so I go home—I don't put the responsibility on you and wait for you to *tell* me to go home.

You will begin to find this inner knowing to be the most precious thing there is in learning to love your neighbor as yourself. There is very little you will have to be told (you won't have to tell me to wear deodorant, because I know how I feel about being pushed to the back far corner of the tram with someone who doesn't) and you'll find that "he who judges himself will not be judged by others."

So first, response. And second, understanding. Third, action. However, "I have to get busy and act," is the cry of the person who thinks he can begin in the Spirit but has to follow up in the flesh. He can't allow this way of responding the freedom to manifest itself in the way it wants to. He must now get in charge.

"But how will anyone know I love them if I don't get busy and show them?" you ask. "How will anyone—the poor or crippled or fat or obnoxious—how will they know I don't look down on them?

And then I remember that some of the blindest people in the world recognized this love in Jesus. "Master," they said, "we know that thou art true and carest for no man: for thou regardest not the person of men, but teachest the way of God in truth."

"You mean it's that simple? It's simply that love *will* reveal itself so people will know?" Sure, it will, just as pride manifests itself. Pride is the overestimation of self, the underestimation of others ("When *I* am sick, I am *sick*. But I know that when *you* get sick, you can take it."). Love is the great leveler. There will be no trace of condescension in the loving person. No trace of "Look how terrific I am not to look down on the handicapped or blacks or fat people." And the rich man—he too will know that I see him as my equal. That I do not feel inferior to him and am not intimidated by him. As you become more and more responsive and seeing, you don't need to concern yourself with applying this love, tearing yourself in fifteen directions all at once. This seeing keeps applying itself to every situation. People are not fools, especially when it comes to picking up on the spirit of arrogance and superiority.

"How can you believe who receive honor one from another?" Jesus asked. And I wondered at this. What did believing have to do with receiving honor from people? Why can't I like the praise of others? Why can't I be a people-pleaser and still believe?

Because believing and receiving honor from other people are opposites. When the children of Israel were dying in the wilderness, Moses was told to raise the serpent of brass and promise that whoever would look at the serpent would be saved. That word "look" and the word "believe" have the same meaning.

Believing is openness. Believing is looking. Caring what other people think about me is "being looked upon"—looking and being looked upon, two opposing orientations. When I care about the opinions of others, my feelings will affect the way I see, while what the Christian sees affects the way he behaves.

Shy children often get involved with spoiled children who use them because the shy child is so conscious of being looked upon that he isn't really looking. He doesn't really weigh the friend's qualities. Doesn't evaluate at all. He just waits for someone, anyone to look on him with favor and is so eternally grateful if someone does that he expects nothing, asks no questions, accepts any kind of behavior. (If a person marries at this stage of the maturing process, he is in for *real* goodies.)

If I care so much about the opinion of others that I can't believe, I'm not hopeless. I simply have to mature, to grow *up* to understanding. When I am given more wisdom, then my priorities will change. Jesus wasn't flattered by the hubbub made over him. He wasn't discouraged because the scribes and Pharisees hated him. He was neither flattered or discouraged, because he understood. He knew what was in man. The fickleness of most of us, the hypocrisy of others.

TEN
JAN RETURNS

I saw Jan a few weeks ago in sweltering 105-degree Texas sunshine and it was like old Alma Mater Day or something. We had a lot of catching up to do, since I'm all but physically incapable of writing a letter, getting an envelope addressed, sticking a stamp to it, and marching it out to the mailbox. The whole job staggers me.

I'd like to report melodramatically that Jan tried to commit suicide following the Munich experience (it'd be so much more interesting), but she didn't. She really didn't. Maybe she has my problem. I seriously thought of suicide one time. The way I remember it now it was between my Zsa Zsa Gabor stage ("I support myself in a way I am accustomed to live and I tell you, dahling, I can barely afford myself") and the Nothing-is-more-important-than-young-love stage when I got jilted. In a fit of delicious self-indulgent misery, I decided to starve myself to death (starvation was the only thing I could think of since I'm deathly afraid of guns and pills). But the plan was quickly aborted by mental pictures of hot, buttery pancakes afloat in maple syrup and Big Macs with cheese dripping and slithering down the side of a huge baked sesame seed bun.

Jan isn't the type to ride the forefront of every new movement with "Truth at Last" blazing from a band around her waist or head, but after she told me that Johnny and the kids were fine she began to talk excitedly (I thought also, profoundly) about the new things she was discovering. She seemed to me like MacDonald's Lilith, who upon entering this "new world" found it her delight, fascination, and enchantment to discover its ways and laws. *Alive* is the only adjective that comes to me at the moment to describe Jan.

The law she was seeing at that time, in nature as well as in the spiritual realm, is that death always precedes real life, not the other way around. As a person dies to his own self-centeredness, he really comes alive. He comes alive in the intended and fullest way just as a seed develops into its intended and fullest way into a flower or tree.

She had once believed in the *theory* that a grain of wheat must die before it comes to life (I suppose even devils believe in that theory), but she was finding out what a difference there is between intellectual "belief" and the understanding or "seeing" that comes through the experience of dying. As she actually began to let go of unimportances (which meant she had to examine the old "shoulds" that governed her life), as she refused to cling to anything in the material or physical world for her delight or security, a new self began to emerge with its own responses, preferences, interests, and way of seeing. This was more substantial than the old self. And less afraid.

She kept saying to herself with each new false promise of fulfillment, "Hey, you can't hang onto that. You're trying to grab on to something that was never meant to be grabbed on to. Everything is a flow. A process."

She was finding out some pretty funny stuff for herself—that the person she thought was *her*, the person with all those whims, that fussy, perfectionist, unhappy person—well, she found that person wasn't a person at all. The ego was never intended to be the real self, but the cocoon containing the self, the cocoon that has to fall away and die before the real self emerges. Then a new creature begins to emerge and shimmer and glisten and gradually unfold and develop out of the old, dry cocoon that you've allowed to die.

Erich Fromm writes: "'To be' requires giving up one's egocentricity and selfishness, or in words often used by the mystics, making oneself empty and poor. But most people find giving up their having orientation too difficult; and any attempt to do so arouses their intense anxiety and feels like giving up all security, like being thrown into the ocean when one does not know how to swim."

I wanted to know if this "reborning" she had mentioned had been a choice for her and she said no, that she had never felt there was any choice in the matter. "I guess it was the marriage thing that did it for me. Marriage was the nice respectable idol that served as my last resort. When I saw I couldn't even cling to one earthly person for my security, the question was then just a very, very weak, To whom shall I go but you? Only you are truth. It was really truth, after all, I was hungry for. I was so weary, so *sick* of falseness and emptiness.

"I saw that all my future happiness depended on the premises, the beliefs I held to and valued. So I've been working on that. At first when I was lonely or afraid I'd cling to a promise like 'Christ will supply all your needs,' cling to it like a drowning man clings to a log. . . . And later I began to see that these ideas need me. They need my thoughts to put their roots down into, to grow, and to extend into other areas of my life — my attitudes — then into the world through new understanding, new attitudes, even a new life-style, would you believe?"

When I questioned her about what she meant by her beliefs changing her life-style, she told me how she had always liked fixing up old houses. This time when she moved back to the

States, wanting all the time possible to be free to read, think, write a little, she and Johnny got the most modern, free-of-care house on the market. She doesn't sew anymore—finds it isn't worth the frustration. She takes all the time the children want to answer their questions, talk with them, and play with them. She's of the firm belief that the only way she can be a happy person to live with is to discover her own deep spiritual needs and make sure they are met. Then she can meet the needs of others out of the overflow.

The most noticeable change in Jan was the absence of what I had felt before to be an awful helplessness. She explained her philosophy—one she felt to be Jesus' philosophy—that life is not an endless series of goals or flights. Isn't a fight-to-the-finish or some kind of war. Isn't a foreordained process in which you have no part. She felt that Jesus pictured life as a quiet, inner process in which the more receptive and responsive we are, the more we give our attention to, dwell on, brood over, and meditate on the laws and premises and promises in the Scripture, the more insight and virtue comes back to us.

As I type this today, I'm filled with a sort of awe at what a miracle this love really is. A miracle because response to God is not something I can will, or decide to do, or learn to do. Response is a gift. But one truth I've been noticing lately is that Jesus didn't try to persuade a person against that person's readiness to fully respond to him. He took it for granted that as long as those he talked to were putting husbands or wives or fathers or lands or traditions or anything else first, they weren't able to respond fully to him.

When certain people or villages didn't respond to the message, as far as anyone knows, Jesus never engaged in idle speculation as to reasons and rationalizations for their lack of response. He never said, "If that village doesn't respond we'll send in a team of psychoanalysts. Maybe the guy's mother died when he was young, or maybe he was tripped down the stairs by a missionary's kid, or *maybe* his grandmother smoked cigars."

Like all responsible people, Jesus drew a clear distinction between my environment and my response to that environment. Jesus contended that every sin has its source—not in the environment—but in my response to the environment. Every sin in the whole catalog of sins is a heart problem, a response problem, a desire problem. The environment can make the problem visible, but it does not create the problem.

The problem originated with the fall of man. Man was never pronounced to be totally depraved. He was pronounced to be dead. Dead to the things of God. And dead means unresponsive, as in the sentence, "My wife is cold and dead toward me, even though she is walking around Hoovering the house." You can be dead to God and still alive to the world. Dead means without desire. Plenty of willpower maybe; plenty of "drive" maybe. But no desire.

What happened at the fall was that man became positively attracted to and responsive to the earth. And without a new heart—well, you know you can clean a pig, give him a sudsy bath, put talcum powder all over him, and take him to town; but if that pig ever sees a mudhole on the way to town, you're in for trouble. He might look just dandy, but you'd better keep away from the mud because he doesn't look at the mud and say "yuk." He, like fallen man, is positively *attracted* to mud.

And that isn't the whole dilemma. We can't do anything to force response. Wagner was the way I found that response is something I can fake, but nothing I can will.

I decide to like Wagner's compositions. My husband likes Wagner. German friends like Wagner. So I am going to try to respond to Wagner's music. I light the fireplace, shine a bowl of apples, make myself comfortable. Now I put my whole self into listening to Wagner. I listen and listen, but pfffft—nothing. I can't respond to Wagner. Something inside of me that handles the business of response doesn't respond to Wagner, and I certainly can't command it to respond. My heart is that very selective something that won't respond to Wagner, and all the head stuff I can think of won't make a dent. I can react to Wagner (get up and turn the awful stuff *off*), but I can't respond.

I find something else. While it's true I can't will response in myself, it's also true that I can't learn to respond or teach another to respond. Marty wanted me to help her discipline her children, and it wasn't long before I saw that Marty's problem wasn't a discipline problem at all. It was a response problem. Her totally incorrigible children, who kick her and yell obscenities at her, walk into the room, demonstrating the above lovable qualities. I sit there staring at Marty a few minutes and then see the ridiculousness of it all. It would be as hopeless for me to attempt to teach Marty how to react to her kids as it would be for me to teach her how to do a knee jerk test. I see that it's my response that determines that I'm incapable of sitting there while a child screams at me or kicks me. I would have to have a gland missing or my hands tied behind my back. I see that inability to respond appropriately in this situation is something, a sickness really, that I can't handle. I can't teach anyone to respond.

I can't learn to respond to God by learning more about him. "To know God is to love him" would only be true if my head and heart were not two separate "people." Knowing someone has much more to do with interpretation of facts which is done by the unconscious "heart" than it does with mere accumulation of those facts. Facts belong to the realm of the head. Interpretation of those facts belong to the realm of the heart. And if there is something wrong with the "heart," then every fact will be distorted and twisted and made to fit in with my basic desire (which in fallen man is always for his own way).

To know facts and to love are two distinct things. You can tell me that God knows all things, but until I feel that God *cares*, I won't be impressed in the slightest. Every fact I know is interpreted by this thing I call my "heart." That's why the person who loves can know you better in five minutes than the person who doesn't love can know you in five years. You can't begin to know until you love because knowing requires sensitivity.

There are other motives for knowing. Knowledge is often motivated by sadism, like the child who "knows" a bird by tearing it apart. Knowledge can be motivated by manipulation—like the woman who wants to know how men tick so she can get what she wants from "her" man. Knowledge can be motivated by the desire to display what we know. But one who seeks to know for those reasons will never truly know another person.

You have to love before you can know. It's like having two children. Two daughters. Both of them know the same facts about you. They both know you have reddish brown hair, that you are at least ten pounds overweight, that you have been known to have a quick temper.

Let's say that one daughter demonstrates love toward you. She actually likes you. Has fun with you. Catches your humor. Catches your meaning. Doesn't twist your words. The other one—well, you do not have the qualities she admires. You don't measure up to her standards. You don't stand up for yourself like she believes you should.

You are ten pounds overweight? The first daughter will probably think something like, "She is kinda nervous and besides, a snazzy shape simply isn't that important to her. So what?" The second daughter will also make her own interpretation of the same fact—maybe something like, "She has no self-control."

And suppose that after years and years of this kind of nonresponse from that daughter who rejects you, you find yourself unable to reveal yourself to her because she misinterprets and twists things. The person who closes God out for a lifetime is going to find himself in the same predicament as the second daughter. "You never knew me" means the kind of knowing that comes through a positive response. The self-righteous rejector will reply, "How can this be? Haven't I done zillions of good works in your name? Haven't I gone to First Baptist Church every week—at least three times?" But eternal life is defined as "knowing God." This is not the static kind of knowing, something you learn about today and which tomorrow is a dead thing. Knowing grows out of response—a real, living, passionate response to the events, thoughts, and experiences that fall on the subconscious processes of the heart.

The very nature of response is that it is always preferential. It is in the nature of response to prefer some things and hate (disregard) others. Shideler writes of man's preferences since the fall: "Indeed, insofar as we remain fallen, we cannot like the good, because to be in sin, original or actual, means to dislike the good."

Why can't I respond to God? After all, he's a person who is warm and kind and perceptive and creative and funny and generous. Why can't I respond to a person like that? Marriage books try to make a principle out of the fact that people (almost always) respond in a predictable way. You treat a man nicely—he will automatically (almost always) respond predictably. Now if this is true in principle, then why doesn't man respond to a God who loves and cares and gives?

Well, the reason husbands and wives don't respond predictably to each other and why we all don't respond predictably to God is because of the nature of fallen man. And the first requirement of stupidity is that you refuse to consider that men and women are in enmity with God, and therefore in enmity with each other.

You can do everything possible for a rejecting unresponsive person and if he is a hostile person, he can't appreciate it. If he's a proud person, he thinks he deserves something better. The rejector wants to misunderstand. He wants to appear to suffer (although he prefers only the *appearance* of suffering, please remember). If something deep inside you is wrong, you want to misunderstand. . . .

Like last Thanksgiving. Gracious German guests serve us American Thanksgiving dinner in their home. After dinner we gather in the living room and our German host casually picks up the newspaper from the mantle. The headlines state that while millions of turkeys had been sold to Americans during this season, there was not one single grateful heart. He reads the headlines aloud dramatically.

The fact that I was a guest in their home prevented me from asking the questions I wanted to ask, "Who went around and checked every American home? How do you check hearts for gratitude? Who, what journalist made this discovery?" The headlines simply reflected the enmity-toward-America in the heart of the journalist who wrote it.

So the problem of enmity, competition, and pride has to be recognized. The proud man cannot care for anyone he cannot look down on (and that only for a very short time). The hostile man, the ambitious competitive man, cannot possibly interpret loving deeds correctly, say nothing of loving motives. To deal with man's enmity, God had to look around for someone big enough to absorb all this hatred and competition and pride into himself, to absorb all of it and yet remain spontaneous and free of hatred. Someone able to actually feel the blows of man's despisings and yet not retaliate. *That* is what the work of God is all about. Love is always costly—and death was the price he paid for man's enmity. We also pay. But that comes later.

ELEVEN
GETTING READY FOR LOVE

One of the questions that had bothered Jan more than any other was why Christians who claim to deal in values seem so celebrity-sick, so stuck on Fun, canned humor, and beautiful people—and why attitudes seem to have no importance to them at all.

The word "attitude" had little meaning to me until I moved to a country where I couldn't understand or speak the language. I was stripped of all words (people couldn't understand me), and others were stripped of words (I couldn't understand them). I began at that point to see how completely I had relied on a person's words to help me form my opinion of that person. If someone told me what a hard worker he was, I would be shocked years later to observe how utterly lazy that person was. After all, hadn't he said, many times, that he was a hard worker?

So, stripped of words, I found myself looking deeper, something I wouldn't have done when well-phrased words impressed me and threw me off and kept me from observing closely. And what I began to see, actually *see*, was something I had never valued in myself or others to any degree of awareness. It's a thing called "attitudes."

When I speak of attitudes, I'm not talking about feelings about yourself, such as confidence, self-respect, etc. I'm talking about your openness or receptivity (or lack of it). And you can't be open if truth isn't your top priority. If you place your children above truth, you will be blind to your children's behavior. If you put one person or group on a pedestal, you won't be open and receptive to the ideas they give out. You won't examine those ideas for the truth in them. You will grab onto any idea your idol gives out and you'll run with it. If you put anything before truth, it's going to affect your reasoning and logic.

For example, if there was one thing I put on a pedestal it had to be intellect. Not intelligence. Not perception. Not insight or understanding. But intellect. Academia. School knowledge. Accumulation of facts—even about God. I placed such a high priority on knowledge that I actually believed that every problem from out-of-wedlock pregnancies to violent crime had to be caused by insufficient education.

One evening something happened that changed my priorities. I had been thinking about the fact that God reveals truth to *every* man. One dares not repress the truth he inherently knows; such repression of truth contributes to immaturity, lack of common sense, and an inability to grow in understanding (since more truth won't be given as long as I'm repressing the truth I already know).

That evening I had been to a group that made me squirm. There's a new person, Rick—right over there—trying to share an insight. Something he was excited about. He speaks falteringly. Shakily. And Joe, who values education, accuracy, and being right, pipes up in a voice that sounds like, "Listen now while God speaks to you"; there is no light or humor behind his eyes. So Joe corrects Rick's inaccurate viewpoint.

Joe tells him he is in the wrong dispensation (I would have sworn *Joe* was living in the wrong dispensation, at least at that moment), and it occurred to me in a flash that the Apostle Peter was absolutely right when he said that the world won't be saved by accurate arguments, but through a certain attitude. Peter called the attitude "submission." We might refer to it today as receptivity or responsiveness or openness.

In this group no one except a specialist was allowed to have an opinion. Attitudes or insight mattered not a drop. These were people who cared about "facts" with no reference to how they perceived or understood those facts. No wonder there was no fresh understanding flowing from the group, since creativity has to do with interpretation. Since truth is not true *to me* until I see it for myself, it was this love of truth, resulting, as it does, in actually finding and seeing truth, that was absent. "Attitudes must be very important to God," was the one thought that summed everything up for me that I'd seen and thought that evening.

I saw that the person who values brains and knowledge and education to the exclusion of this subjective receiving side of his own self is actually denying polarity—the two poles being the gift of love (the Word of God) and the gift of faith (the ability to receive the meaning known to be hidden in the message). This person is not only ignoring his own subjective side, but actually despising it—and therefore despising himself.

We never come to know each other or God or anything through evaluation and analysis and taking things apart, but only through revelation and receptivity—through love and faith. My interpretation of St. Paul's "scandalous" teachings about the woman keeping silence in the Church is that he wanted to picture and explain these two poles—penetration and reception. The male represents the first by his work of preaching, giving out the message, and sharing the revelation. The woman represents the second by receiving, interpreting, bearing fruit of that cold knowledge that was planted. To say that the seed is more important or the soil is all-important is to say that growth is unimportant—because both knowledge and understanding are required for synthesis and growth.

Only after seeing the importance of faith—one's attitude—did the overbearing, authoritarian style become intolerable to me. I began to feel as if I was in a nursery. I wondered how it had happened that I, a person God had made a priest, was not adult enough to face the bleak and barren prospects of grappling with truth (or even playing with it and having fun with it). I could only laugh at such condescension: "Here, open your mouth. One more bite. Daddy will tell you the meaning, the interpretation."

This is why early believers demanded repentance. "Unless you change your *way* of thinking you will not enter the kingdom" was how Jesus suggested that my own lack of objectivity has the power to prevent others from seeing what is there.

While Christians don't all believe exactly alike, they do share in a certain way of thinking, just as earthly families often do. The Browns. Remember the Browns? Remember in high school when you broke up with Chester Brown, every Brown in the state turned up their collective nose at you as you walked by? You even found yourself flunking algebra (a third cousin of Chester's great aunt taught algebra). It was always "the Browns against the world" and what you found out when you broke up with Chester was that you were once again part of the world the Browns hated.

The Browns came to mean to you a whole way of thinking. A closed, secretive, defensive, all-for-one-and-one-for-all way of thinking. On the other hand, Christian thinking begins with a word used often by early believers (a word almost eliminated from modern vocabularies)—*repentance*.

Before I could understand why Repentance 101 was the essential requirement for the life of love, I had to understand the difference between head and heart, and between will and desire. While God wills, plans, and acts on his will without man's consent, God also desires that all men consent to come to him. But God does *not* act on even that desire without man's consent.

Now, I think, repentance has nothing to do with feeling bad or shedding tears or intending to do better or even changing behavior. Repentance isn't something I do, but rather could be defined as "Readiness to pay the price for love." Repentance is not the condition of salvation (which is an accomplished fact). It is the state I must reach before I am free to believe and before God will accept me (somewhere modern believers have picked up the idea that God has no choice but to accept anyone who comes to him whether they are repentant or not).

The requirement of "repentance" or readiness can be seen in the male-female relationship. "Becoming one flesh" in marriage was based on the requirement that the man emotionally give up his past and cleave to his wife (while the immature man protects his parents and his past and criticizes and rejects his present—his wife and children). "Becoming one" was known to require the giving up of one's securities. This price of emotionally leaving one's past is not the price paid for love (love is still the one thing you cannot buy), but it is the price one pays to be *free* to love.

If you profess to love me, to want to marry me, and yet I find every moment of your time full, your home full of other women, I know you do not love me. You are not ready to pay the price of love.

I also had to recognize that each thing in life, by simply being what it is, has certain requirements. I can go to the store for a large green beach ball and the lady may only have a small orange beach ball—but that's okay. I'll take it. It's fine. But if she goes into the back room and brings me out a square object—no matter if it is large and green—I'd have to reject the square object on the ground that a ball has certain requirements in order for it to remain a ball. The same principle applies in marriage. If marriage is "a mutually exclusive sexual relationship between a male and female," then one of the requirements for a marriage to remain a marriage is sexual fidelity.

All the old saints have confirmed this truth of love's requirement. Bonhoeffer says in *The Cost of Discipleship:* "The light of the body is the eye and the light of the Christian is his heart. But the heart is dark when it clings to earthly goods, for then, however urgently Jesus may call us, his call fails to find access to our hearts. Our hearts are closed, for they have already been given to another."

There is Pascal: " 'I would soon have to renounce pleasure,' say they, 'had I faith.' For my part I tell you, 'You would soon have faith if you renounced pleasure.' Now it is for you to begin. If I could I would give you faith. I cannot do so, nor therefore test the truth of what you say. But you can well renounce pleasure, and test whether what I say is true." By pleasure, Pascal wasn't referring to watching *Gangbuster* reruns — but the all-consuming pleasure found in one's own way of living life.

The concept of "grace through faith" differentiates between the gift of grace and faith (the attitude one takes toward this love). If I am hanging onto the past, if I have my hands full, I do not have faith. George MacDonald defined faith this way: "Do you ask, 'What is faith in Him?' I answer, the leaving of your way, your objects, your self and the taking of His and Him; the leaving of your trust in men, in money, in opinion, in character, in atonement itself. . . . I can find no words strong enough to serve for the weight of this obedience."

TWELVE
LOVE: A WAY OF SEEING

The growing person has begun to be aware of new desires and interests. This he is probably expecting. But something very unexpected then begins to develop. He begins to notice something no one ever told him about. A new kind of intelligence is beginning to develop in him. Not head intellect, but something called heart intelligence—the heart that broods over, dwells on, and wonders about principles. Like Lilith, he finds himself in a marvelous new world where it is assuredly his business to discover its ways and laws.

"But what does intelligence have to do with *love?*" I asked myself when I first began to notice this new thing in me, having grown accustomed to the soft, flabby definition of love-as-a-feeling. I had grown used to thinking of Christian mentality as a passive thing like nodding your head sleepily and saying, "Uh-huh, go on."

My discovery—that love matures into a certain kind of keen intelligence—is explained by St. Paul: "I pray that your love may abound yet more and more and extend to its fullest development in knowledge and all keen insight . . . that is, that your love may display itself in greater depth of acquaintance and more comprehensive discernment. So that you may surely learn to sense what is vital and approve and prize what is excellent and of real value—recognizing the highest and best."

Jesus identified the nature of conversion as insight or discovery, rather than as a decision or choice. "You are the rock," Jesus said to Peter after Peter's exclamation that Jesus was the Christ that was to come. "Upon this rock I will build my church." What was Jesus talking about? What was he identifying as the bedrock of real conversion, the rock on which his kingdom was to be built?

Jesus told us plainly what this rock was. It wasn't Peter. Wasn't the Church. Wasn't Peter's confession. "Flesh and blood has not revealed this to you, Simon Bar-jona, but my Father . . . he has revealed it unto you." The rock was personal revelation. Insight into the mysteries of God. (A mystery, by the way, isn't something incomprehensible—it is simply truth not discoverable by human reason.) It was this gift of personal revelation (along with Peter's receptive faith which was capable of receiving such revelation) that was the rock.

This love, this insight isn't static, but grows and matures. My friend tells me how her love has matured. "Let me tell you where I was fifteen years ago," she offered once.

"Gee, I don't know. What is this going to be—true confessions or something?"

"I'm serious," she assures me. "I had—what do you call it—accepted Jesus. But it was a purely intellectual thing. I was an empty person, by which I mean I hadn't really cared enough about important things to understand much of anything or to reach any kind of authentic viewpoint."

I must have been looking at her strangely, because I couldn't imagine this woman having *ever* been lacking in understanding of spiritual things, or lacking in originality. She reminded me of the fulfillment of the promise, "Out of their inner beings will flow springs of living water."

"Anyway," she continues, "I had talked myself into being in love with this fifty-two-year-old guy who had been through three ex-wives (the one I knew looked at least seventy-five years old, probably from her short encounter with him). He had at least five children who hated the sight of him. He was an artist, the misunderstood variety, with a drinking problem. But I fell hard. I was still so immature I thought love was a matter of trying to see something good in everyone, and putting it there if I couldn't see it.

"I've noticed that the dishonest person lets how he feels about someone affect what he sees (rather than the other way around). I spent two years being what I thought of then as 'understanding,' telling him how cruel life was to him, how no one understood his great genius, how super-talented he was, how terrifically good-looking he was. . . .

"One morning he called, asking me to meet him at the Bayrishcher Hof. I phoned in 'sick' at my office, even though we were wild with work and I had to stay late for a week to make up for it. There my wonderful lover sat across from me at the dining table. He ordered us both meals that would have delighted the pickiest connoisseur with money I knew one of his penniless college-aged sons would have been delirious to have, when suddenly he informed me that we must rush through dinner because his new girl friend from Frankfurt was coming in on the 2:45 plane. My heart stopped (did he really *say* what I thought he said?) and I went home with my eyes open for the first time—only because this time he was doing *me* dirty.

"Well, after a few days of dragging myself around, feeling sorry for myself, I realized there is nothing else to love but truth — that the only object love can possibly have is truth, that love is loyal to truth before it is loyal to people. Just then I caught a reflection of myself in the C&A department store window. Was that *me*, schlepping along with no makeup, in a pair of old sloppy brown loafers that looked like bedroom slippers? What was I *doing* to myself? How did I *dare* put the word *love* on this blindness I had suffered from, on this fantasy that created a wonderful person out of a selfish, uncaring, luxury-loving bore?"

My friend, you see, had been raised by fawning, unperceptive parents who couldn't see through manipulation or lies or deception. "They were the intellectual type," she explains, "always rationalizing even the most gross behavior. I wonder," she had mused aloud, "I wonder if the worst result of all this was this feeling I had that because my parents (though intellectual) could not see, then other people could not see. And that in turn led to the conclusion that God does not see."

I have no idea if her explanation was correct, but if so, maybe this is why she had to be converted through a man whose values were so right-on that he could see through her pretenses and bluffs and manipulation. She tells me that it was this very quality of perception in this man, his whole way of seeing and perceiving that made her realize that God sees. That God sees all. That God can't be manipulated, "cutied" into doing the things she wanted him to do for her. It was her first entrance into the fear of God.

She says she felt like a blind person whose sight was suddenly restored. She was embarrassed and ashamed because she realized that all these years while she had been blind, unseeing, she herself had been visible to others. She had been seen. Unable to edit and control what others had seen.

In front of this man with the Awful Perception, this man who could penetrate through her pretenses, who wasn't impressed with her beauty or her money, she suddenly knew this was how God saw her. Not impressed in the slightest. But — well, "pity" was the word she used.

This friend had known lots of people who knew how to quote the Bible — some of the most unperceptive, dull people she had ever known. (The whole brown dress, brown bun-on-the-nape-of-the-neck business.) But this woman had never before known the difference between knowledge and perception. Or between head knowledge and heart intelligence. Her bafflement reminded me of what St. Paul had said on the subject: "The spiritual man has insight into everything, and that bothers and baffles the man of the world."

C. S. Lewis wrote: "Love gives a power of seeing . . . to see, in some measure, like God. His love and his knowledge are not distinguished from one another, nor from Him. We could almost say he sees because he loves. . . ."

Spiritual perception is a progressive thing. Christians I bump into seem to have gone through a pretty definite pattern of discovery. There is the recognition of who Christ really was, the recognition of the inability of the human will to do anything, the recognition of what God's grace implies, and on and on. The miracle of this work within me is described by Tozer in *Born After Midnight:* "For a man to understand revealed truth requires an act of God equal to the original act which inspired the text."

Is this new kind of intelligence a gift — given only to certain Christians? One morning I woke up, aware for the first time that God actually puts the person who knows the things of God (the Holy Spirit) within me, within every Christian, and that the Holy Spirit *is* the gift underlying all gifts. That the Holy Spirit actually reveals truth to everyone who wants this gift (not to the one who wills, but to the one who desires).

Remember the promise you would have filed under *H* for Heaven? The one about "Eye has not seen nor ear heard, neither have entered into the heart of man the things that God has prepared for them who love God"? But then I see something new. Hey, this promise isn't about heaven. It's a now kind of thing—ending with the reminder that even though eye has not seen, etc., God has revealed those things to us. I get a new glimpse of my work—receiving. And God's work for me—revealing.

This seeing changes me. Rollo May in *Existential Psychology* writes: "We can demonstrate at every moment of the day in our psychotherapeutic work that only the truth that comes alive more than an abstract idea and is 'felt on the pulse'. . . . Only this truth has the power to change a human being."

St. Paul had another word for the person who is lacking in spiritual intelligence. That word was carnality. He makes it clear that there are three classifications of men, all three classes relating to the person's attitude toward and perception of the things of God. There is natural man, to whom the word and work of God are foolish. There is spiritual man, who is able to receive all truth (even though the receiving and comprehending of reality is a lifelong process). And there is carnal man, who has an inability to receive deeper truth. The carnal man lacks comprehension of spiritual principles and the nature of God. He can learn only elementary truths, but can't digest deeper truth.

Carnality is embarrassing. A carnal Christian took an agnostic friend of ours to dinner for the purpose of encouraging him to join his church.

"Why should I join?" this friend finally asks.

"Because of the Man upstairs," Simple Simon answers.

"You mean God, of course?"

"Well, yes. The way I feel is that you'd better get all the points you can with the Man upstairs—uh, God," he urges fervently.

His victim across the table looks at him coldly. "Maybe you

could brush up on your beliefs," he suggests. "Christians believe a man is saved by grace, not by works."

"If I loved people I could just accept what they think and not care," someone said recently, a woman who believed herself to be a positive thinker. "Gee," I plead, "if you see me tottering on the edge of a cliff, I hope you'd tell me. If your love has quality and intelligence and depth to it, you'll care *more* about my thinking. It will matter more, not less."

"The spiritual person judges the value of everything," Paul writes. God isn't pleased with my "devotion" if he knows quite well that I have no perception, no spiritual intelligence, not the slightest appreciation of good, or the slightest trace of hatred for evil.

Maybe it's a little like if I painted landscapes and you came to look at them and told me how you love, how you *adore* my painting, how much my painting techniques have improved. I won't be happy with your compliments and professions of love for my paintings if I know very well that you understand nothing about art, even to the extent that you "decorated" your living room with flowered green wallpaper, purple-flowered carpet, orange, overstuffed furniture with pink doilies pinned on the arms and back.

Purely human love is blind. A teen-ager dropped her boyfriend a while back and her eyes were opened about the nature of human love. Her boyfriend loved her until she quit loving him, at which time he began doing all kinds of vindictive things (like slitting the tires of her car). He had never really *seen* her, but had loved her only because he thought she was *his*. One day he had claimed to see all kinds of lovely qualities in her; the next day, when she no longer was his possession, he despised her.

The only way I knew God loved me, the only way I *felt* that love was to know I was fully and completely seen—and still loved. When people used to say, "God loves you in spite of the way you are" (which, to me, meant "in spite of the fact that you are no good"), I would yawn and say something like, "That's nice." What I really meant was "So what?"

But when a man of God said, "God loves you because God sees. God sees what you don't see. He sees your worth." I intuitively knew that to be real love. I jumped to my feet and said, "Hey, I wonder if that's true? If that's true, that's really something!" I couldn't go to sleep very quickly that night. I wondered what it was God could see that he considered worthwhile enough to die for. It was the beginning of my self-esteem (which is the opposite of self-righteousness).

Worth is not created by people. You don't create worth by telling a person how wonderful he is, hoping he'll live up to your expectations and become more "worthwhile." Because of the kind of life you have in you, you simply have an "eye" for the worth already there. It's like when I go junk-shopping for furniture to refinish. What I'm looking for is something salvageable. Something that is *there* at that moment (*not*, for heaven's sake, what some people refer to as "potential," which means something like "What you will be someday when I get through working on you and polishing you up"). I'm looking for something *there*, even beneath two coats of yuk green or putrid yellow paint. I buy the piece of furniture I know has present worth—solid cherry or maple or oak beneath all the crud—and I spurn the plastic and fiberboard, even though that may look much better.

One of the large banks of America has a short film out, warning managers not to loan to anyone who has bad credit not due to accidental causes.

A man who saw this film was upset. "Don't people believe in forgiveness anymore?" he asks.

"You can forgive a person's behavior if he steals from you or won't pay you back what he owes you, but only God can forgive a man's way of thinking. Perpetual bad credit indicates not a few isolated slips, but a whole unrealistic way of thinking, and unless this is changed, he and everyone involved with him will get in the same mess again and again."

In *Psychology Today*, Michael S. Serrill contends that any real prison reform will come about only through a whole new way of thinking. New prisons or new television sets or better food aren't going to make a dent. He says that criminals aren't the products of society, victims of circumstances like abuse and deprivation (the conventional view), but according to his sixteen-year study he reports that criminals can be spotted at an early age according to certain very definite errors of thinking. One error: "It is better to be under the sod than not to be God." Another: they rejected authority before authority ever rejected them—they were victimizers, not victimized. Another: in spite of the crimes and injuries they commit, they all believe themselves to be good, decent persons.

Paracelsus wrote, "He who understands nothing is worthless. But he who understands also loves, notices, sees." King David wrote something very similar: "He that understands not," he warns, "is like the beast that perisheth."

Truth is not something you tell. It is a whole way of thinking and perceiving. It begins in a child in the seeing of self-evident facts (that an intelligence has made the world, for example), and later comes to receive clear revelation of primary spiritual laws, primary facts which can't be reduced further (the seeing, for example, that love is never "won," never earned, but that it is given freely).

Wisdom is actually realistic thinking, seeing things as they are, from God's point of view. Wisdom is seeing objectively, not competitively. (James points out that the competitive spirit is wisdom's antithesis.) I saw this when I went with a neighbor to see a house of a friend. It's a razzle-dazzle kind of house. We stand and gape and compliment. "What a snazzy house," I say on the way home. My neighbor is quiet. "Now

I don't want to go home to *my* crummy house," she pouts. It wouldn't do me any good to point out that she, herself, has a lovely home. She has a competitive spirit. She has seen this house not as an objective fact, but only in comparison with her house. Love and competitiveness are at opposite ends of the pole.

Love-as-a-way-of-seeing is not primarily concerned with this material world; it is not concrete-bound. When Timothy writes of the God "who wishes all men to be saved and increasingly to perceive and recognize and discern and know precisely and correctly the divine truth," he is referring to a person involved with principles and propositions and promises.

Faith receives, wonders at, and searches out reality. "You become original by seeing things as they are," a former art teacher once told our class.

"But reality is what *is*: trees, flowers, butterflies, dirt, problems, . . ." said a student who took great pride in the fact that he saw more porno movies than anyone in the class. This, he thought, made him more realistic than others ("After all—that's reality! That's how real people live!").

"Reality isn't what is. Reality is what is *so*," the teacher pointed out. "A dirty street *is*—it exists—but it isn't reality. A smutty story *is*—it exists—but it isn't reality. Reality is what is *so*. As a man sows, so shall he reap—that's reality. Before you can really live you must die—that's reality."

"And truth? What is truth?" I want to know.

"Truth is a personal experience of meaning. It is when what is so becomes real to me. When I see it for myself."

Why does God reveal truth to some and not to others? Does it have to do with how hard you think? Never. It has to do with how receptive you are to the Word. Just recently I was explaining to one of the children why I had made the statement that the Word of God has power.

"It has life in itself," I explain. "I notice it's a lot like a seed you plant in the ground. It's this *seed* that bears fruit of itself, the Word of God that does the thinking in me. All I have to do is give the Word the room in my thoughts to grow, to think, to expand, to come to consciousness. And giving it this kind of attention, it thinks in me."

What is the only thing that lasts forever? Feelings don't. Knowledge doesn't. Habits don't. Faith doesn't even last forever. Faith discovers Reality, principles, what-is-so. But what-is-so lasts longer than the faith that discovers it. Reality, principles—the Word of God—stands forever.

What is the object of faith? Can you have faith in the visible? Can you have faith in visible things, like big crowds coming to your church, or a gold Cadillac? No, you can trust in them, value them, believe in them, but you can't have faith in them. You can only have faith in something invisible, the invisible that is always behind the visible. ("By faith we see that that which is seen is made by that which does not appear.") If you can see something, you don't need to have faith in it.

You need faith (openness to God) to receive the Word of God, not a high IQ. And the Word of God doesn't appear to us in some Casper-the-Ghost form that we "invite into our hearts." The Word of God comes to us in the form of propositions identifying fundamental truths. When the eye of faith perceives such a proposition, it requires no proof or explanation—all of your proofs and explanations will spring from this new thing you have seen.

You can't see principles like "What a man sows is what he'll reap." You can't see that right away. You don't smoke a cigarette and zap, cancer. Reaping what you sow is actually a principle you have to have faith in, and if you really "see" it, if you really "get" it, it is *truly*, as James declared, going to change your behavior.

But how about people who claim they have prayed for certain tangible things like money or cars or houses and have received them? Are they feeding us a line? Or is it true that what they were *really* having faith in, if it was real faith, wasn't money or a gold Cadillac at all? If they have real faith, what they had faith *in* was some principle or proposition like "God provides all your needs," or "God is good," or "Seek first the kingdom and all these things will be added unto you."

Reality (what-is-so) is to believed, and faith lays hold on those propositions, receives them into itself, broods over them, lets them germinate in the soil of the heart, and finally realizes, sees, and perceives the meaning that was hidden to the eyes before. This new intelligence comes about through remaining an open person — not through straining or trying to memorize or hard thinking. This is why the meek will inherit the earth. Dag Hammarskjold wrote of his goal: "To remain a recipient and be grateful. Grateful for being allowed to listen, to observe, to understand."

Jesus' parables, like all symbols and images, require faith that believes there is meaning and substance in those simple stories, a faith that believes that the mysteries of the ages are hidden in them. Through this faith we know that what is true in the physical world is true in the spiritual — that the spiritual becomes understandable through the physical. The man who believed Christ would heal his servant had faith. He saw that what was true for him (he, himself, could tell his servant to go and he would obey) was also true in the spiritual world. Christ said of this man's faith that he had never seen anything to equal it in all of Israel.

This man didn't just "happen" to have faith. This kind of practical understanding of the spiritual is only given to the person who wants it, just as wisdom was given to Solomon because he wanted wisdom before he wanted anything else in the world.

Kind, compassionate Meister Eckhart wrote something that

would sound outlandishly cruel to the man who is unaware that the spiritually ignorant person is ignorant because he *wants* to be ignorant. He wrote: "There are people who have the name of being saintly on the basis of external appearances, but inside they are asses because they don't grasp the meaning of divine truth."

When I use the word "see" or "perceive" I suppose you know I do not mean "to see wholly and completely." Now, in this life, we see in part, as through a dark glass. But at least love sees. Love gives seeing to the person who is not an either/or person. Such a person would rather see in part than not at all. To those who say, "All life is to be a mystery," to the extent that they refuse to look and open themselves and see—they turn love away.

To those searchers for meaning on the other hand, well, it's like what Jan said about this new inner intimacy she's found: "Another day to observe, listen, notice, care, come to conclusions. Maybe to reap understanding of things that have been planted long ago and have been germinating in the dark." This inner place is where love begins—where earth and seed struggle with each other in the darkness—and out of this synthesis of opposites Truth (the child of Love) springs forth into Awareness.

LIST OF BOOKS

Berdyaev, Nicolas. *The Destiny of Man.* New York: Harper & Row, 1960.
Bonhoeffer, Dietrich. *The Cost of Discipleship.* New York: Macmillan, 1967.
Branden, Nathaniel. *The Disowned Self.* New York: Bantam, 1973.
Fromm, Erich. *To Have or To Be?* New York: Harper & Row, 1976.
Gardner, Herb. *A Thousand Clowns.* New York: Random House, 1962.
Lewis, C. S. *Abolition of Man.* New York: Macmillan, 1962.
―――. *Grief Observed.* New York: Seabury, 1963.
MacDonald, George. *Phantastes and Lilith.* Grand Rapids: Eerdmans, 1964.
May, Rollo. *Existential Psychology.* New York: Random House, 1961.
―――. *Love and Will.* New York: Norton, 1969.
Pascal, Blaise. *Pensees.* New York: Penguin, 1966.
Perls, Frederick S. *Gestalt Psychology Verbatim.* New York: Random House, 1971.
Rand, Ayn. *The Romantic Manifesto.* New York: New American Library, 1971.
Reik, Theodor. *Listening with the Third Ear.* Moonachie, NJ: Pyramid Publications, 1972.
Rogers, Carl R. & Stevens, Barry. *Person to Person: The Problem of Being Human.* Moab, UT: Real People Press, 1967.
Tozer, A. W. *Born After Midnight.* Harrisburg, PA: Christian Publications, n.d.
Weil, Simone. *Waiting for God.* New York: Harper & Row, 1973.